THE
COMMERCIAL
WOODS
OF
AFRICA

A DESCRIPTIVE FULL-COLOR GUIDE

PETER PHONGPHAEW

Linden Publishing Co. Inc.
Fresno, California

THE COMMERCIAL WOODS OF AFRICA
By Peter Phongphaew

All photos by Peter Phongphaew
Cover design by James Goold

135798642

Printed in Singapore

Library of Congress Cataloging-in-Publication Data

Phongphaew, Peter.
 The commercial woods of Africa : a descriptive full color guide / by Peter Phongphaew.
  p. cm.
 Includes bibliographical references and index.
  ISBN 0-941936-82-1 (alk. paper)
 1. Wood—Africa. I. Title.

TA419.P56 2003
674'.1'096—dc22

2003016409

Linden Publishing Inc.
2006 S. Mary
Fresno CA
www.lindenpub.com

TABLE OF CONTENTS

ACKNOWLEDGEMENTS

I would like to give special thanks to the following people who made the implementation of this book possible:

John S. Kotiram, Dara-Foret, Mangina (D.R. of the Congo)

Saj Jivanjee, Portland, Oregon, USA

Rolf Klemme, Texwood Trading, Meerbeck, Germany

Leslie C. Mullican, Portland, Oregon, USA

C. Henning Wolters-Fahlenkamp, Bruchhausen-Vilsen, Germany

Georg Kraemer, Timber Technical High School, Bad Wildungen, Germany

Dr. Hans Georg Richter, University Hamburg, Federal Scientific Institute of Timber Biology, Germany

J. Timothy Warren, Portland, Oregon, USA

Dieter Zange, Blumenau, Santa Caterina, Brazil

I wish to also extend my appreciation to Kent Sorsky and Richard Sorsky of Linden Publishing, Fresno, California, USA, and to Richard Kuehndorf, Rejean Drouin, Henk Bakker, and Alan Curtis. Finally, I would like to offer my thanks to all of my many friends and colleagues who helped me along the way.

—Peter Phongphaew

INTRODUCTION

It is the purpose of this book to provide a much-needed survey of African commercial timbers. This concept was developed through the author's own experiences and connections with the timber industries in Africa, Asia, Europe and North America, whereby it has become clear that most timber brokers, merchants, and marketers lack sufficient access to information about African woods. This book, therefore, is meant specifically for the members of the wood trade. It is not a scientific work designed to provide exhaustive technical details, but is rather a book of pertinent information collected about the most important, commercially-viable African woods.

Graceful Muhimbi trees.

OUTLOOK FOR WORLD FOREST PRODUCTION AND CONSUMPTION

It is estimated that between 1996 and 2002, the worldwide volume of forest production increased at a rate of 1.7 percent per year. This trend is expected to continue through 2010, at which time overall production will be equivalent to about 1.87 billion cubic meters (792 billion board feet), some 25 percent higher than that of

1999. In 2010, Asia, Europe and North America together will constitute about 85 percent of global forest production and represent more than 90 percent of consumption; while North America will remain the single largest producing, importing and exporting region, its rate of future growth will be slow compared to areas with still-developing timber industries such as Asia and South America.

POSSIBLE MARKET EVOLUTION

Many tropical countries are developing the means to export processed wood products as opposed to merely shipping out cut logs. This trend could lead to a drop in the export of semi-finished products in favor of goods with a higher added value. In Africa, countries such as Ghana, Ivory Coast, Cameroon, Uganda, Kenya, Tanzania, South Africa, Mozambique, Republic of Central Africa, Togo, Benin, and Nigeria have either begun to implement or have already established this capability.

Another issue is that in the future, the volume of timber harvested in exploitable natural forests could diminish for two reasons. Firstly, owing to the increased importance accorded to ecological concerns, some tropical countries with significant forest reserves have decided to restrict the quantity and scope of the harvesting permits they issue; others will likely follow their lead. Secondly, the volume harvested should logically diminish as logging is increasingly done in already-exploited forest tracts and less frequently in virgin forests.

The output of tree plantations should comprise the majority of the potential increase in production in forthcoming years, as it would seem that few countries will be able to increase their natural forest production in a sustainable manner.

Harvesting timber in the Democratic Republic of the Congo.

AFRICAN TIMBER EXPORTS TO EUROPE, ASIA AND NORTH AMERICA

At a time when timber consumption and production are increasing across the world, the total volume of legal African timber exports has declined in recent years—from about 5 million cubic meters (2.1 billion board feet) in 1995 to some 3.25 million cubic meters (1.4 billion board feet) in 2000. This striking 35 percent decrease is largely a result of Africa's erratic political climate, where civil wars and unstable governments severely impact economic productivity. One facet of Africa's export woes is its meager penetration of the huge North American market. For example, in 1995 African nations exported 2.2 million cubic meters of sawn timber (.93 billion board feet), with just 13 percent of that total reaching the U.S. market.

There is a definite need for a well-prepared collaborative effort to promote African tree species, to spur timber production, and to increase exports to both the American and world-wide markets. Cooperation between Europe, Africa, Asia and North America is needed to develop an international marketing campaign for African timber, the purpose of which would be to bring greater visibility and accessibility to the continent's commercially interesting woods. Additionally, cooperative efforts could bring necessary investment and improvements to areas such as infrastructure, education, the exchange of experiences and information about commercial tree species, environmental concerns, and forestry maintenance and reforestation.

For example, the development of tree plantations in Africa is one area where international assistance is extremely beneficial. These plantations are a relatively new and underutilized component of the African economy, and there is a large

Wood cutting shed.

role for private foreign investors to work with local companies or governments to fund or oversee their creation.

A specific instance of this activity is how European scientific institutes have assisted in experimental reforestation projects in Ivory Coast that have yielded good results. Special nurseries are prepared for the planting season (March/April); in 1999, for example, 490,000 seedlings were prepared in order to reforest 528 hectares (2 square miles). The majority of these seedlings consisted of rapid growing species (teak, fuma, okume) in balance with the various forest species (bete, koto, makore, khaya-mahogany) and fruit-bearing species (cola, olive). The resultant tree density was about 210 plants per hectare.

Additional efforts such as this where international entities coordinate with local ones to pursue economic objectives should be continually encouraged.

A NOTE ABOUT THE AFRICAN CONTINENT

The African continent is the poorest of the world, and the people of Africa have suffered greatly from both continuing internal strife and exploitation by foreigners in the forms of slavery and the theft and destruction of natural resources. African timber has often been a source of special interest to outsiders, who have in the past cleared whole forest regions and effectively devastated the pre-existing natural environment. All too frequently, the local human inhabitants, in addition to their forest habitat, were destroyed.

Thus the critical question arises: how best should those in the timber industry deal with the forest economy of Africa? How should local populations be integrated into the process of developing and managing an efficient infrastructure for the timber industry? How can these same people be made to be intimately involved in the crucial task of reforestation and the maintenance of natural resources? A commitment must be made by all parties involved, be they individuals, organizations, corporations, or countries, who partake in the commercial exploitation of Africa's forest resources to take the responsibility for implementing the concepts required to bring forth a future of prosperous, sustainable economic activity.

A village in the Congo.

AN OVERVIEW OF AFRICA

GEOGRAPHY

Africa is the world's second largest continent; with a surface area of approximately 30 million square kilometers (11.6 million square miles), it is three times as large as Europe. The Sahara Desert, which itself is slightly larger than the continental United States, comprises almost one-third of Africa's land mass. The tropical zone is extensively forested and includes the enormous Congo River Basin which contains almost 20 percent of the planet's rain forests. Major transitional regions exist between the rain forests and the Tropics of Cancer and Capricorn. Over 800 million people, or approximately 13 percent of the world's population, live in Africa.

FOREST FORMATIONS

Most of the timber species treated in this book can be found in Africa's closed canopy evergreen rain or damp forests (the designation *damp forest* is increasingly used in place of *rain forest*). It should be noted that there does not exist a uniform definition of what constitutes a tropical or subtropical rain forest formation, with worldwide literature defining a number of different terms and designations. However, all definitions tend to agree upon the following characteristics: rain forests receive almost constant rain and usually have a (relatively) dry period of fewer than two months; annual rainfall amounts to something in the range of 1700 mm (67 in). The temperatures which accompany precipitation normally range between 24–30 degrees Celsius (75–86 degrees Fahrenheit). The vegetation itself actually never changes. The wood volume usually varies between 250–300 cubic meters (106,000–127,000 board feet) per hectare, but in extreme cases can be as much as 800 cubic meters (339,000 board feet). Evergreen rainforests exist in Central Africa between 5 degrees of northern latitude and 5 degrees of southern latitude; they are also found in West Africa along the Gulf of Guinea between the coast and 7–8 degrees of northern latitude.

To the north and south of the rain forest are the less thickly vegetated forests of Africa's great tropical savannah zone. These are populated by deciduous trees, and receive somewhat less rainfall than the rainforests. Other forest or tree formations found in the progressively drier regions of the continent are of little relevance to the tree species described in this book.

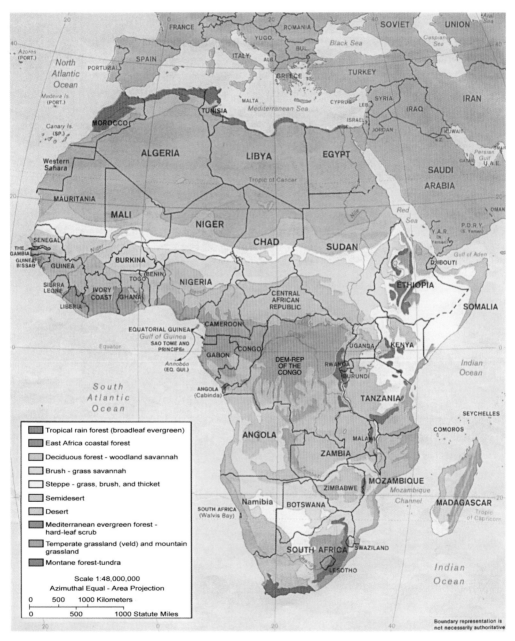

Natural vegetation in Africa.

TIMBER EXPORT SPECIES

There are an estimated 2,000–2,500 different tree species in Africa, although only a small percentage are of commercial interest. The tree composition of each region substantially differs. The *Meliaceae* family (which contains approximately 750 species around the world) provides the largest proportion of exportable timbers, including, among others, African mahogany and woods such as sipo, sapelli, kosipo, avodire, dibetou, tiama, and bosse clair. The *Leguminosae* family is even larger, but in terms of exportable woods is second to *Meliaceae*. Examples of commercial *Leguminosae* timbers (which are normally heavy woods) include dabema, afzelia, ebony, grenadill, limbali, muhimbi, padouk, wenge, zebrano, bubinga and movingui. Various types of soft woods such as emien, essessang, kumbi, aiele, cordia, effeu, fuma, obeche, and okume are exported as replacements for pine, cedar and spruce. However these exports are often unprofitable because of the long and expensive transportation routes involved.

The Ituri Forest in eastern Democratic Republic of the Congo.

POLITICAL CONSIDERATIONS OF FORESTRY IN AFRICA

One high-profile aspect of the African timber export industry is the tropical wood boycott movement, sponsored in large part by Green political parties, as well as environmental groups in Europe, North America and elsewhere such as Greenpeace and Robin Wood. These entities and others concerned by the destruction and degradation of tropical forests, legal or otherwise, hope through means of a boycott to diminish logging activity by suppressing foreign demand for tropical woods.

Commercial, governmental, and environmental interests have attempted to resolve their differences through a variety of means; these efforts have taken many forms, and each country tends to have its own approach. A major new idea has been the implementation of certification programs designed to guide and reward ecologically sustainable logging activities in tropical countries. The World Wildlife Fund through its Forest Stewardship Council (FSC) operates the single largest certification program. FSC-approved timber products are certified as having been produced according to sound, sustainable forestry principles. Countries and companies are encouraged to sell and purchase only FCS certified timber products.

In addition to the FCS program there are other forest certification projects, some of which are backed by law. However the concept of certification is not without controversy, often lacks a sufficient structure to resolve disputes, and has not been adopted by many countries and companies.

MECHANICAL PROPERTIES

Each tree description in this book includes a table of mechanical properties (defined below). These values are generally based on a moisture content of 15–20 percent; however, some very heavy woods such as grenadill, ebony, and bongossi may have moisture content levels as high as 35 or 40 percent.

Certain values may be absent for trees about which relatively little is known and for which sufficiently rigorous testing has not yet been performed. On a related note, as those familiar with African woods can attest to, those values and properties which do exist are subject to change based on observation, experience and further testing. Some of the species which the European market was long familiar with are no longer available and have been replaced by other species which have not been used for a sufficient length of time to determine with certainty their characteristics and best applications. It is hoped that if African woods better penetrate the North American market, additional testing will be performed and our knowledge of these timbers will increase.

Durability class: Fungal decay or rot is the primary cause of wood deterioration over time. Therefore it is important to establish a system of classification to indicate the degree of durability (or resistance) a wood has against fungal decay. A durability class (I–V) signifies the approximate natural life expectancy of a wood before decay compromises its structural stability. More precise estimates concerning the life expectancies of individual woods cannot be given, as site conditions present too many variables to account for. Note that the life expectancies listed below reflect circumstances where the wood is in contact with the ground; this is the optimal condition for fungal decay to occur (resulting in the shortest life expectancy).

class	definition	life expectancy under moderate climactic conditions	life expectancy under tropical climactic conditions
I	very durable	25+ years	15+ years
II	durable	15–25 years	10–15 years
III	moderately durable	10–15 years	5–10 years
IV	low durability	5–10 years	up to 5 years
V	not durable	2–5 years	less than 1 year

Raw density: This measurement specifies the relationship of a wood's weight to volume. The unit of measurement is grams per cubic centimeter (g/cm^3). Increasing raw density brings with it a noticeable improvement in general characteristics and physical properties such as hardness, durability, heat conductivity, and swelling and shrinkage values. The often useful measurement of specific gravity (the comparison of a wood's density to that of water) is also easily determined. Water's density is 1 gram per cubic centimeter. Therefore, a wood with a raw density of .5 would have a density 50 percent less than that of water.

classification	raw density (g/cm^3)	English equivalency (lbs/ft^3)
light	under .4	under 24.96
medium	.4–.7	24.96–43.68
heavy	over .7	over 43.68

Note: in the English system of measurements, water has a density of 62.4 lbs per cubic foot.

Bending strength: This measurement specifies the amount of bending force required to cause wood to break. The unit of measurement is Newtons per square millimeter (N/mm^2). The bending strength values in this book were determined by using small wood samples in their originally-cut dimensions. Bending strength improves as hardness increases and wood moisture decreases; bending strength may also be influenced by the grain and by wood formations such as knots and burls.

classification	bending strength (N/mm^2)
very low	under 50
low	50–85
medium	86–120
high	121–175
very high	over 175

Compression strength: This measures a wood's level of resistance to breaking from applied body stress (i.e. its crushing strength). The unit of measurement is Newtons per square millimeter (N/mm^2). A wood's compression strength value is always based on a test of its horizontal strength; when appropriate, a vertical compression test (a lateral bending of the fibers) is also performed and its value is combined with that of the horizontal test to derive a single number. Compression strength improves with increased raw density and reduced wood moisture.

classification	compression strength (N/mm^2)
very low	under 20
low	21–35
medium	36–55
high	56–85
very high	over 86

E-module: This value refers to a wood's stiffness, or modulus of elasticity. The unit of measurement is Newtons per square millimeter (N/mm^2): $e = 1N/mm^2 = 1Mpa$ (megapascal). While subject to the effects of compression stress, a wood's positive or negative elasticity is tested by slowly loading material onto one point in the wood (elasticity is mostly examined parallel to the grain or fiber to reflect typical real world usage patterns). This testing may be supplemented by dynamic tests using ultrasonic, resonant frequency or acoustic oscillation methods.

classification	e-module (N/mm^2)
low	under 10,000
medium	10,000–15,000
high	over 15,000

Volume dwindle: This value measures the reduction in volume of wood that has undergone kiln drying and is expressed as a percentage of the original volume. Shrinkage along the longitudinal, radial and tangential directions are all represented in this figure. A low volume dwindle value is generally preferable. Note that after being dried, wood may re-absorb a certain amount of water and experience a slight increase in moisture content.

classification	volume dwindle (%)
low	less than 5%
medium	5–10%
high	over 10%

Tangential and radial shrinkage: These values measure (in percentages) the change in length between wet and dry wood. These values assume a wood sample that has a more or less uniform level of wood moisture throughout. Shrinkage results may be different if certain sections of a piece of timber are notably drier than others before the drying process commences.

classification	radial shrinkage (%)	tangential shrinkage (%)
low	under 3%	under 2%
medium	3–6%	2–5%
high	over 6%	over 5%

METRIC/ENGLISH MEASUREMENT SYSTEM EQUIVALENCIES

1 mm	0.039 in	1 cm	0.394 in
1 m	3.281 feet	1 km	0.621 mi
1 cbm	423.78 board feet	1 ha	2.471 acres
1 inch	25.4 mm	1 inch	2.54 cm
1 foot	.305 m	1 mile	1.609 km
1 bd ft	0.00236 cbm	1 acre	0.405 ha

DESCRIPTIONS OF APPLICATIONS

Construction wood: General construction wood usable for a variety of projects including the construction of buildings, bridges, halls, balconies, water engineering construction, or other uses requiring heavy timber elements.

Furniture: Various furniture products including solid-wood furniture, glued furniture elements, cabinet doors, and industrially manufactured furniture.

Flooring: Solid wood flooring, heavy foot planks, industrial parquets, glued parquets, special floors for sports facilities.

Walls, decking: Boards or planks for external walls for houses or other buildings; decks and balconies, fences and other similar outdoor carpentry projects.

Paneling: Wooden panel elements for indoor walls, ceilings and related surfaces.

Intarsia works: All manner of intarsia works (floors, panels, works of art, etc.).

Musical instruments: Wood usable for the body or frame, or constituent components, of musical instruments.

Cabinetmaking: High-quality manually-crafted (or partially-manufactured) cabinets and similar pieces of furniture.

Plywood: Plywood, plywood sheets or layers, packing material, crates and excelsior.

Doors: Solid-wood doors, industrially manufactured and glued doors, door components, door fillings for plastic coated doors; various other types of portals.

Staircases: Solid-wood stairs; typically for home use.

Window frames: Wooden or combination wood-plastic window frames.

Laboratory furniture & fittings: Woods with a good level of acid resistance are useful for the production of laboratory furniture and containers.

Ship, rail & truck building: Wood components for transportation: boat building, railroad cars, truck loading docks.

Weapons industry: Wood components—such as gunstocks—used to manufacture weapons.

Rotary cut veneer: Rotary cut veneer slicing.

Flat sawn veneer: The wood is cut flat and converted to a thin veneer; usually used for furniture.

Blind veneer: Veneers that usually serve as glued interior layers of plywood; non-decorative purposes.

Modeling: Various artistic or hobby uses, do-it-yourself woodworkers, model construction, etc.

A note about maps: The purpose of the small habitat maps that accompany each wood description is to indicate regions where there exist commercially exploitable concentrations of the timber. The tree may well be found in other areas not indicated on the map.

DESCRIPTIONS OF WOODS

ABURA *(Hallea ciliata or Mitragyna ciliata)*

Family:	*Rubiaceae*

Other Names:	*bahia*
Cameroon:	*eliom, mukonia*
Ghana:	*subah*
Uganda:	*nzingu*
D.R. of the Congo:	*vuku maza*
Ethiopia:	*woda*
Belgium:	*longwa*

HABITAT
Abura is abundant in West African rain forests, and less frequently found in East Africa. Its preferred habitat is near rivers and in flood regions.

TREE DESCRIPTION
The abura is a medium-sized tree with a height of between 30–35 m (98–115 ft) and a diameter of between 60–90 cm (2–3 ft). Its fibrous bark is approximately 2.5 cm (1 in) thick. The timber-suitable section of the trunk is straight and cylindrical, with only a small amount of above-ground roots.

WOOD DESCRIPTION
Abura sapwood is approximately 10 cm (4 in) thick and is a bright pinkish-gray color. The core wood is slightly darker, and can further darken over time, changing from light to dark brown. The wood is somewhat opaque and possesses a very straight, fibrous structure with fine pore grooves. On occasion the tree may grow in a twisting fashion. Very old abura trees may be hollow at the core.

Durability Class	III	**E – Module**	10,900 N/mm^2
Raw density	0.56 g/cm^3	**Volume dwindle**	12.5 %
Bending strength	78 N/mm^2	**Tangential shrinkage**	8.3 %
Compression strength	43 N/mm^2	**Radial shrinkage**	4.2 %

PROPERTIES AND APPLICATIONS

The wood has weak physical properties, but can be easily cut and processed; drying is typically a straightforward procedure. Abura is used in the production of plywood and acid containers (acids do not damage it). It is also used by cabinetmakers, and is a good substitute for birch, beech and alder.

USES

Indoor

Very Good	Good	Usable	Not Usable
plywood	furniture	flooring	construction wood
	walls, decking	intarsia works	musical instruments
	paneling	doors	ship, rail & truck building
	cabinetmaking	window frames	
	staircases	weapons industry	
	laboratory furniture & fittings	rotary cut veneer	
	flat sawn veneer		
	blind veneer		
	modeling		

ADONMOTEU / KIBAKOKO *(Antonatha fragrans)*

Family: *Caesalpinaceae*

Other Names:
Liberia: *side-doa*
Ivory Coast: *hounouio, teoulebape*
Cameroon: *ekobem*
Congo countries: *kibakoko, boleka,*
                      bulimbusa, empoposo,
                      libuundukulu,
                      watsangila

HABITAT
Adonmoteu (also commonly known as kibakoko) grows in tropical rain forests; its habitat extends from Sierra Leone into the Congo basin and south to Angola.

TREE DESCRIPTION
A large evergreen, the adonmoteu ranges between 25–30 m (82–98 ft) in height and 60–80 cm (2–3 ft) in trunk diameter. However, exceptional specimens may be as tall as 40 m (131 ft) and as much as 130 cm (4 ft) in diameter. The lower portion of the trunk is only slightly cylindrical, with irregularly developed root buttresses.

WOOD DESCRIPTION
The 15 cm (6 in) thick sapwood, with its pale white to yellowish-gray color, is clearly differentiated from the brownish copper-colored core wood (in younger trees the core wood may be a lighter yellowish-brown with irregularly veined brown-violet stripes). The wood texture is medium-rough.

Durability Class	III	E – Module	15,400 N/mm^2
Raw density	0.76 g/cm^3	Volume dwindle	13.7 %
Bending strength	117 N/mm^2	Tangential shrinkage	8.9 %
Compression strength	72 N/mm^2	Radial shrinkage	4.8 %

PROPERTIES AND APPLICATIONS

Adonmoteu wood is hard and heavy, yet quite flexible; it possesses good strength values and is weather-resistant. The core wood is moderately durable and exhibits a tendency to warp during drying. It can be used to produce decorative flat sawn veneers, and is a recommended raw material for any manner of artistic carpentry projects. Adonmoteu's range of applications is similar to limbali (*see separate listing*), although the latter possesses superior physical characteristics.

USES
Indoor/Outdoor

Very Good	Good	Usable	Not Usable
	construction wood	weapons industry	musical instruments
	furniture	rotary cut veneer	plywood
	flooring		laboratory furniture & fittings
	walls, decking		blind veneer
	paneling		modeling
	intarsia works		
	cabinetmaking		
	doors		
	staircases		
	window frames		
	ship, rail & truck building		
	flat sawn veneer		

AFRORMOSIA *(Pericopsis elata or afrormosia elata)*

Family:	*Papilionaceae*
Other Names:	*kokrodua*
Ghana:	*kokrodua, mohole*
Ivory Coast:	*assamela*
Nigeria:	*ayin*
Cameroon:	*ejen*
Rep. of the Congo:	*ole pardo*
D.R. of the Congo:	*wahala, bohala*

HABITAT
Afrormosia is a rare tree species found in West and Central Africa, including the countries of Ivory Coast, Nigeria, Ghana, Cameroon, and the Congo states. The tree grows primarily in groups.

TREE DESCRIPTION
Afrormosia is a large tree reaching heights of 30–50 m (98–164 ft). The straight and cylindrical trunk is 60–160 cm (2–5 ft) in diameter, and is clear of branches for up to 30 m (98 ft). The scale-like bark is fibrous with strong red marks.

WOOD DESCRIPTION
The sapwood, about 3 cm (1.2 in) thick, is a lightly-colored mixture of white, green, and yellow. The core wood is greenish-brown with a silky luster and often displays greenish-red stripes. Pores may be filled with tannin, which can form calcium marks.

Durability Class	I	E – Module	12,500 N/mm²
Raw density	0.75 g/cm³	Volume dwindle	9.8 %
Bending strength	140 N/mm²	Tangential shrinkage	6.0 %
Compression strength	70 N/mm²	Radial shrinkage	3.5 %

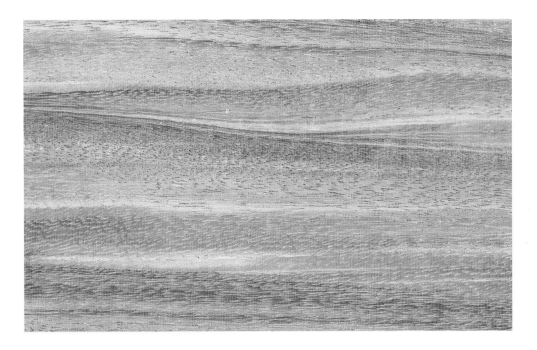

PROPERTIES AND APPLICATIONS

Afrormosia is a fine, heavy wood, harder even than teak (*Tectona grandis*), and is often used for decorative work. It possesses good physical properties and is highly resistant to damage and insect attack. It is a popular choice for veneers; note that for such applications the wood must be well-steamed and worked on while hot, and that cooled-off blocks must be reheated before resuming work. Afrormosia veneer can be used for high-quality parquets, panels, and furniture. If it is to be used outdoors, the wood should be treated with polyurethane; for indoor use, Nitrocellulose lacquer is the appropriate treatment.

USES

Indoor/Outdoor

Very Good	Good	Usable	Not Usable
furniture	musical instruments	construction wood	plywood
flooring	doors	staircases	window frames
walls, decking	modeling	ship, rail & truck building	laboratory furniture & fittings
paneling		weapons industry	blind veneer
intarsia works			
cabinetmaking			
rotary cut veneer			
flat sawn veneer			

AIELE *(Canarium schweinfurthii)*

Family:	*Burseraceae*
Other Names:	*canarium*
Rep. of the Congo:	*m'Bil, bayombi*
D.R. of the Congo:	*safukala, mbidikala*
Sierra Leone:	*mbili*
Liberia:	*goekwehn*
Ivory Coast:	*labe*
Ghana:	*bediwunua*
Nigeria:	*elimi*
Equatorial Guinea:	*olem*
Gabon:	*olivi*
Uganda:	*mwafu*

HABITAT
Aiele is found along the entire Gulf of Guinea coast, from Sierra Leone to Angola, and also deep in the Congo basin up to the shores of Lake Victoria. These trees are spread throughout the evergreen forest and frequently exist in the transitional region of the humid savannah zone.

TREE DESCRIPTION
This species reaches heights of up to 50 m (164 ft). The lower segment of the trunk is buttressed by short, small, downward sloping roots. The branchless section of the trunk is cylindrical and often grows to more than 150 cm (5 ft) in thickness and 20 m (66 ft) in height.

WOOD DESCRIPTION
The color of the trunk ranges from pink to ruddy red. The thick sapwood and core wood are similar in appearance: the sapwood is yellowish-white, while the core wood tends to be grayish-white (and may also have a pink sheen).

Durability Class	IV	E – Module	8,400 N/mm^2
Raw density	0.49 g/cm^3	Volume dwindle	11.7 %
Bending strength	65 N/mm^2	Tangential shrinkage	7.1 %
Compression strength	42 N/mm^2	Radial shrinkage	4.4 %

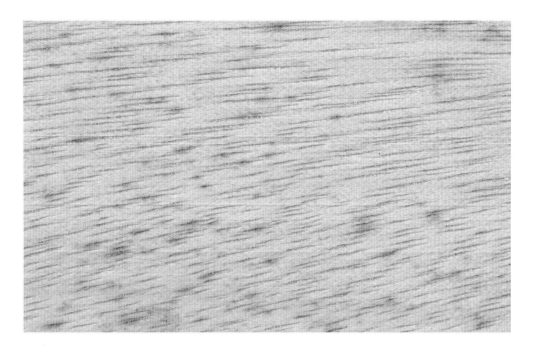

PROPERTIES AND APPLICATIONS

The porous, moderately-soft wood is considered quite workable, although it cannot be used in bending or twisting processes. Aiele is brittle and subject to the formation of fissures. Despite these weaknesses, the wood is a favorite export and is frequently processed into a sealant for veneers. It possesses good staining properties and is used for plywood production in Europe; in addition, it is used in the manufacture of imitation mahogany products.

USES

Indoor

Very Good	Good	Usable	Not Usable
plywood	rotary cut veneer		construction wood
blind veneer	flat sawn veneer		furniture
	modeling		flooring
			walls, decking
			paneling
			intarsia works
			musical instruments
			cabinetmaking
			doors
			staircases
			window frames
			laboratory furniture & fittings
			ship, rail & truck building
			weapons industry

ALEPZPE *(Albizzia coriaria)*

Family: *Mimosaceae*

Other Names:
D.R. of the Congo: *alepzpe*

HABITAT
Alepzpe is largely unknown to the outside world. Unlike other *Albizzia* varieties which are found growing in groups throughout much of tropical Africa, this tree grows individually and only in the Ituri region of the eastern Congo.

TREE DESCRIPTION
This slim tree has a maximum trunk diameter of 100 cm (3.3 ft), and achieves heights of approximately 20–25 m (66–82 ft). The trunk is straight with up to 15 m (49 ft) of timber-usable wood; there are smallish above-ground roots around the base. The crown of the tree is spherical with a sparse canopy of leaves.

WOOD DESCRIPTION
The wood is light-brown, sometimes partially yellowish, with short wavy stripes. It yields a golden gloss after being dried with an artificial light.

Durability Class	IV	E – Module	6,000 N/mm²
Raw density	0.55 g/cm³	Volume dwindle	-
Bending strength	-	Tangential shrinkage	-
Compression strength	-	Radial shrinkage	-

PROPERTIES AND APPLICATIONS

Alepzpe has few proven uses as little formal testing of its physical properties has been performed. Its physical beauty makes it a good candidate for veneer production. The wood dries and peels well. However, alepzpe is susceptible to weather and insect attack and should be given a standard chemical treatment before shipment.

USES

Indoor

Very Good	Good	Usable	Not Usable
	rotary cut veneer	furniture	construction wood
	flat sawn veneer	walls, decking	flooring
		paneling	intarsia works
		cabinetmaking	musical instruments
		plywood	doors
		blind veneer	staircases
		modeling	window frames
			laboratory furniture & fittings
			ship, rail & truck building
			weapons industry

ANTIARIS *(Antiaris africana)*

Family: *Moraceae*

Other Names: *ako*
Cameroon: *diolosso*
Ghana: *chenchen, barkclothtree*
Nigeria: *oro, ogiovu*
D.R. of the Congo: *bonkonko*
Gabon: *andoum*

HABITAT
Antiaris trees inhabit much of West Africa, from Senegal on the Atlantic coast eastward to the Congo region. The species grows primarily in rain forests but is also found growing in groups in the savannah. It is a rare presence in the highlands, where it only exists individually, separate from others of its kind.

TREE DESCRIPTION
Antiaris grows quickly, and can reach heights of up to 40 m (131 ft), with diameters ranging from 70–90 cm (2.5–3 ft). The trunk, which develops in a straight and cylindrical fashion, provides up to 20 m (66 ft) of usable wood. There are well-formed root buttresses.

WOOD DESCRIPTION
The sapwood and core wood are identically colored. The wood has a grayish-white to yellowish-brown color, frequently displaying beautiful, decorative stripes. Freshly cut wood has an unpleasant smell which disappears upon drying.

Durability Class	IV	E – Module	8,500 N/mm²
Raw density	0.45 – 0.55 g/cm³	Volume dwindle	11.5 %
Bending strength	68 N/mm²	Tangential shrinkage	7.1 %
Compression strength	36 N/mm²	Radial shrinkage	4.4 %

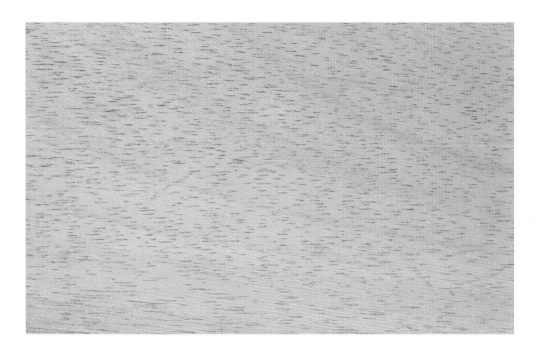

PROPERTIES AND APPLICATIONS

This wood has good mechanical and physical properties, and is easily cut and machined. The drying process does not cause notable difficulties; however, the wood is prone to becoming bent or wavy. Antiaris is not weather resistant and is very susceptible to insect attack. It can be peeled while fresh, without first being steamed. Antiaris is often used for blind veneers (interior plywood layers), while other applications include use as packing wood for shipping and as a replacement for cork.

USES

Indoor

Very Good	Good	Usable	Not Usable
plywood		walls, decking	construction wood
rotary cut veneer		paneling	furniture
blind veneer		intarsia works	flooring
		cabinetmaking	musical instruments
		flat sawn veneer	doors
		modeling	staircases
			window frames
			laboratory furniture & fittings
			ship, rail & truck building
			weapons industry

AVODIRE *(Turraeanthus africana)*

Family:	*Meliaceae*
Other Names:	*African goldbirch*
Ghana:	*apapaye, wansenwa*
Cameroon:	*engan*
D.R. of the Congo:	*esaw, lusamba, ndango*

HABITAT
Avodire is found in coastal regions along the Gulf of Guinea, including the countries of Ivory Coast, Ghana, and from Cameroon to Angola. The tree normally grows in sandy soil, apart from others of its species, although in Cameroon and the Democratic Republic of the Congo, it often grows in groups.

TREE DESCRIPTION
Avodire is a medium-sized tree which can attain a height of 35 m (115 ft) and a diameter of 60–90 cm (2–3 ft). The trunk is clear of branches up to 15 m (49 ft), and has no visible roots at the base; there are often holes in the lower half of the bole. The tree has a tendency toward irregular growth, frequently twisting and turning. After felling, the bark must be quickly removed in order to avoid trunk decomposition.

WOOD DESCRIPTION
The sapwood and core wood have a similar coloration, although the core wood develops a yellowish- or brownish-gold color upon exposure to air. Faint stripes of irregular dimensions may be present. Avodire resembles the Asiatic Ceylon satinwood, and belongs to the African mahogany family.

Durability Class	III	**E – Module**	10,100 N/mm^2
Raw density	0.55 g/cm^3	**Volume dwindle**	11.6 %
Bending strength	106 N/mm^2	**Tangential shrinkage**	6.5 %
Compression strength	80 N/mm^2	**Radial shrinkage**	3.8 %

PROPERTIES AND APPLICATIONS

Avodire is hard and solid, possessing good technical and physical properties—superior even to oak. The wood dries quickly and without difficulty and is easily processed. It should be pre-drilled for nailing. Avodire is very susceptible to humidity and insect attack and is therefore suited for indoor purposes only. It makes a beautiful furniture veneer and is a popular choice in the flooring industry, as well as with the production of pianos, paneling, and luxury furniture.

USES
Indoor

Very Good	Good	Usable	Not Usable
furniture	musical instruments	plywood	construction wood
flooring	staircases	doors	window frames
walls, decking	weapons industry	blind veneer	laboratory furniture & fittings
paneling	modeling		ship, rail & truck building
intarsia works			
cabinetmaking			
rotary cut veneer			
flat sawn veneer			

AZOBE / BONGOSSI *(Lophira alata)*

Family: *Ochnaceae*

Other Names:
United Kingdom: *ekki, red ironwood*
Sierra Leone: *hendui, kokank*
Spain: *akoga, okoka,*
                    palo de hiero
D.R. of the Congo: *bonkole*

HABITAT
Azobe (commonly known as bongossi in Europe) is found mainly in damp ever-green and tropical sump forests ranging from Guinea-Bissau to the Congo, with its largest concentrations being in Cameroon and Equatorial Guinea. It is found in groups and only rarely as an individual tree.

TREE DESCRIPTION
Azobe reaches heights of up to 50 m (164 ft), with diameters between 70–140 cm (2.5–4.5 ft). There is no above-ground rootage, giving the tree a straight, cylin-drical appearance. It is free of branches for up to 30 m (98 ft) and has a small, spherical crown.

WOOD DESCRIPTION
The sapwood is about 5 cm (2 in) thick and whitish-pink to grayish-brown in color. The core wood is chocolate-brown to violet-brown, darkening to blackish-brown after exposure to air. An interesting characteristic of this wood is the tran-sition from the sapwood to the core wood—this area is an approximately 8 cm (3 in) thick zone that is a mixture of colors and different fiber structures.

Durability Class	I	E – Module	24,000 N/mm²
Raw density	1.07 g/cm³	Volume dwindle	16.4 %
Bending strength	190 N/mm²	Tangential shrinkage	8.7 %
Compression strength	109 N/mm²	Radial shrinkage	7.4 %

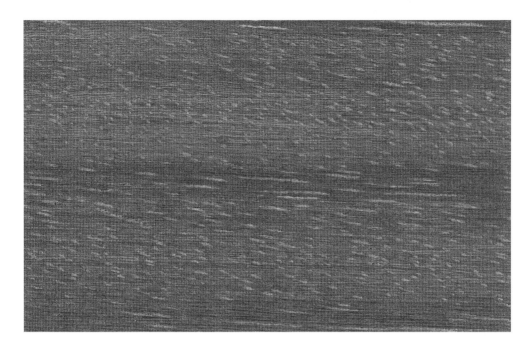

PROPERTIES AND APPLICATIONS

Azobe is firm and heavy, being amongst the hardest usable woods in the world, and is largely impervious to the effects of insects and weather. These qualities make it a first-class construction timber with tremendous longevity. However, drying must be done slowly, and at low temperature, to avoid breakage or distortions. Examples of Azobe's many uses are bridge construction, the building of railway sleepers and freight cars, and vehicle construction. In addition, it is used for wood decking, heavy lumber beams, and the production of laboratory furniture.

USES
Indoor/Outdoor

Very Good	Good	Usable	Not Usable	
construction wood	rotary cut veneer	furniture	laboratory furniture	
ship, rail &	flat sawn veneer	flooring	& fittings	
truck building		walls, decking	weapons industry	
		paneling	blind veneer	
		intarsia works	modeling	
		musical instruments		
		cabinetmaking		
		plywood		
		doors		
		staircases		
		window frames		

BETE / MANSONIA *(Mansonia altissima)*

Family: *Sterculiaceae*

Other Names:
Ghana: *aprono*
Nigeria: *afon, ofun, odo, urodo*
Rep. of the Congo: *kuol*

HABITAT
Bete (commonly referred to as mansonia) grows in coastal regions stretching from Liberia to Cameroon, as well as in the Congo basin. It thrives in rain forest zones that have distinct dry seasons.

TREE DESCRIPTION
This tree species is typically about 35 m (115 ft) in height with a diameter of 50–80 cm (1.5–2.5 ft), although larger specimens have been found in Cameroon. The trunk is cylindrical and clear of branches for up to 20 m (66 ft); minimal root buttresses may be present. The white-brown bark will burst apart on older trees; local people are known to extract poison from it for arrows.

WOOD DESCRIPTION
The white sapwood is 4 cm (1.6 in) thick and has no useful applications. The color of the core wood is generally olive to violet-brown but can vary between magenta with gray-green strips and violet. Its appearance is similar to American black walnut (*Juglans nigra*). The drier the wood, the more even the color and grain; the fiber is generally very even. Bete trees may have crystalline deposits of calcium oxalate in the pores of the core wood.

Durability Class	III	E – Module	13,000 N/mm²
Raw density	0.60 – 0.70 g/cm³	Volume dwindle	11.9 %
Bending strength	125 N/mm²	Tangential shrinkage	6.2 %
Compression strength	60 N/mm²	Radial shrinkage	4.0 %

PROPERTIES AND APPLICATIONS

Bete is a medium-hard and moderately heavy wood. It is stable, flexible, shockproof, and possesses a high bending strength. It is easily machined, good for splitting, and has physical characteristics that allow drying with very little twisting. The wood has a medium level of durability and, because of its toxic contents, a long life. Bete wood is used for musical instruments, cabinetmaking, flooring and children's furniture. It is also highly suitable for the veneer industry.

USES
Indoor

Very Good	Good	Usable	Not Usable
	flooring	construction wood	plywood
	walls, decking	furniture	laboratory furniture & fittings
	paneling	doors	ship, rail & truck building
	intarsia works	staircases	
	musical instruments	window frames	
	cabinetmaking	weapons industry	
	flat sawn veneer	rotary cut veneer	
		blind veneer	
		modeling	

BILINGA *(Nauclea diderrichii)*

Family:	*Rubiaceae*

Other Names:

Ivory Coast:	*bedo, ekusamba*
Ghana:	*kusia, kusiaba*
Nigeria:	*ppepi*
Cameroon:	*akondoc, eke*
Rep. of the Congo:	*n'gulu, mokesse*
D.R. of the Congo:	*mokese, linzi*
Uganda:	*kilingi*

HABITAT

Bilinga is a light-wood species that exists in remote areas of humid evergreen forests, damp lower plain zones, and riverbanks. Its habitat extends across Central Africa from Guinea to the Congo region.

TREE DESCRIPTION

Bilinga reaches a height of 25–40 m (82–131 ft) and has a diameter of 70–180 cm (2.5–6 ft). If root buttresses are present, they will be small in stature. The tree grows in a mainly straight and cylindrical manner, although twisting patterns are not uncommon. Bilinga bark excretes a clear, bitter juice, which is used in the pharmaceutical industry.

WOOD DESCRIPTION

The wood has a lemon-yellow color which quickly darkens upon exposure to light, taking on a glossy orange-red to gold-brown color. The sapwood is light in color, approximately 4 cm (1.6 in) thick, and has no uses. The core wood is solid, with a somewhat rough texture and short fibers.

Durability Class	II	E – Module	12,800 N/mm^2
Raw density	0.76 g/cm^3	Volume dwindle	12.8 %
Bending strength	107 N/mm^2	Tangential shrinkage	8.0 %
Compression strength	65 N/mm^2	Radial shrinkage	4.7 %

PROPERTIES AND APPLICATIONS

Bilinga is a heavy and physically strong timber, although it has a tendency when felled to crack at the core. The wood splinters easily, but responds well to gluing. Its resistance to fungus, insects and weather is an advantage. The timber is quite suitable for the manufacturing of furniture and paneling and can produce a beautiful grain for flat sawn veneers. In general, bilinga is a good choice for solid wood construction.

USES

Indoor

Very Good	Good	Usable	Not Usable
flooring	furniture	construction wood	musical instruments
flat sawn veneer	walls, decking	intarsia works	plywood
	paneling	cabinetmaking	ship, rail & truck building
	doors	staircases	weapons industry
		window frames	blind veneer
		laboratory furniture & fittings	
		rotary cut veneer	
		modeling	

BOIRE *(Detarium senegalense)*

Family:	*Ceasalpiniaceae*
Other Names:	*tallow tree*
Liberia:	*kolei, kpay*
Gabon:	*alen*
Sudan:	*tambacoumba*
Ivory Coast:	*bodo*
Nigeria:	*ogwega*

HABITAT

Although *Detarium* species can be found from Senegal to the Sudan, the boire variety is itself very rare. It grows individually in damp Central African forest regions and at the edges of coastal zones. Most exports of this timber originate from Ivory Coast.

TREE DESCRIPTION

Boire is a medium-sized tree up to 30 m (98 ft) in height, with a diameter between 80–120 cm (2.5–4 ft). The trunk grows in an uneven, non-cylindrical manner, and the segment of timber that is free of branches is only about 9 m (30 ft) in length. The bark is grey and 25–30 cm (9.8–11.8 in) thick. Boire resembles the Khaya tree, and when mature bears some resemblance to a pyramid.

WOOD DESCRIPTION

The white-rose colored sapwood is approximately 7 cm (2.8 in) thick. The core wood is dark reddish-brown with a violet gloss (planed surfaces show this gloss very clearly).

Durability Class	III	**E – Module**	10,000 N/mm²
Raw density	0.67 g/cm³	**Volume dwindle**	12.4 %
Bending strength	77 N/mm²	**Tangential shrinkage**	6.3 %
Compression strength	38 N/mm²	**Radial shrinkage**	4.9 %

PROPERTIES AND APPLICATIONS

Boire is a homogeneous, heavy wood, and bears recognizable similarities to palissandre (*see separate reference*) and other members of the *Dalbergia* family. It has a pleasant-smelling resin which, during processing, can make cutting and sawing more difficult. Although Boire dries well, it is subject to being torn. Decorative veneers of this wood are popular in the furniture industry; note that to produce flat sawn veneers, the wood must first be thoroughly steamed so as to imbue it with moisture and heat. Boire is also popular for processing as solid wood, particularly in the parquet industry. It should only be used for interior purposes since humidity can harm its outward appearance.

USES
Indoor

Very Good	Good	Usable	Not Usable
furniture	flooring	construction wood	musical instruments
intarsia works	paneling	walls, decking	plywood
cabinetmaking	weapons industry	doors	window frames
flat sawn veneer		staircases	ship, rail & truck building
		laboratory furniture & fittings	blind veneer
		rotary cut veneer	modeling

BOSSE CLAIR *(Guarea cedrata)*

Family: *Meliaceae*

Other Names:
Ivory Coast: *krasse*
Ghana: *kwabohoro, bossi*
Nigeria: *white guarea, obobonofua*
Cameroon: *ebangbemva*
D.R. of the Congo: *bosasa, lisasa, bosse fonce*

HABITAT
Bosse clair is found in the evergreen rain forests between Liberia and Uganda. It grows individually, and rarely in groups.

TREE DESCRIPTION
This large tree species can reach heights of up to 50 m (164 ft) and diameters of up to 120 cm (4 ft). The trunk's surface is grooved. The bole is straight and cylindrical and is clear of branches for up to 28 m (92 ft). The roots of larger bosse clair trees are visible above the ground.

WOOD DESCRIPTION
The wood is brownish-pink with white-yellow sapwood. The core wood will eventually darken to a reddish-brown color after being cut and dried.

Durability Class	II	**E – Module**	11,800 N/mm²
Raw density	0.55 – 0.65 g/cm³	**Volume dwindle**	9.0 %
Bending strength	94 N/mm²	**Tangential shrinkage**	5.3 %
Compression strength	50 N/mm²	**Radial shrinkage**	3.6 %

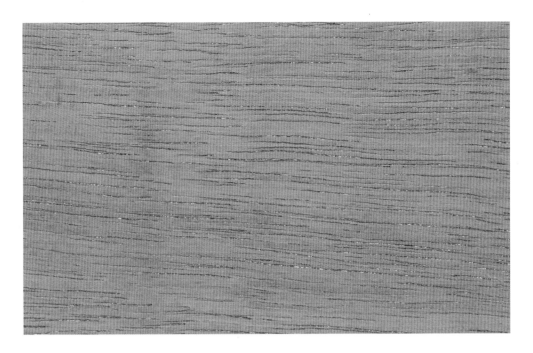

PROPERTIES AND APPLICATIONS

This moderately heavy wood possesses high elasticity and fair dynamic strength properties. It is popular with large furniture manufacturers (especially for piano-making and chair production), and is commonly used for home and window frame construction. The kiln drying process must be carefully attended to since the wood tends to crack, thereby causing some blocks to sweat out resin. Otherwise, the wood is considered quite durable and weather resistant.

USES

Indoor/Outdoor

Very Good	Good	Usable	Not Usable
furniture	construction wood	intarsia works	plywood
	flooring	ship, rail & truck building	blind veneer
	walls, decking	weapons industry	modeling
	paneling	rotary cut veneer	
	musical instruments	flat sawn veneer	
	cabinetmaking		
	doors		
	staircases		
	window frames		
	laboratory furniture & fittings		

BUBINGA *(Guibourtia tessmanii)*

Family:	*Ceasalpiniaceae*

Other Names:
Cameroon:	*essingang, okweni*
Gabon:	*ovang*
Congo countries:	*waka*

HABITAT
Bubinga exists in much of West Africa, where it flourishes in humid, swampy areas, growing either alone or in small groups. In Gabon, the rare and little-used *Guibourtia pellegriniana* variety is found.

TREE DESCRIPTION
Bubinga trees are 20–45 m (66–148 ft) in height. The straight and cylindrical trunk has a diameter between 80–160 cm (2.5–5.5 ft), and is free of branches for up to 20 m (66 ft). The base is typically buttressed by high, strong roots.

WOOD DESCRIPTION
The sapwood is yellowish-white and up to 7 cm (2.8 in) thick. The core wood is rose-pink brown to dark violet. The wood has a fine, fixed structure and will often display a multi-colored quality or have dark, beautifully-colored stripes.

Durability Class	II	**E – Module**	13,000 N/mm^2
Raw density	0.92 g/cm^3	**Volume dwindle**	14.1 %
Bending strength	140 N/mm^2	**Tangential shrinkage**	8.6 %
Compression strength	70 N/mm^2	**Radial shrinkage**	5.3 %

PROPERTIES AND APPLICATIONS

Bubinga has good static and dynamic physical properties. It is flexible and impact-resistant and, although very hard, is quite suitable for processing. The wood dries slowly but without difficulty. Applications for bubinga include luxury veneers, intarsia work, paneling, and molding work. It is worth mentioning that this wood produces a resin, kopal, which is an important raw material for lacquer production.

USES

Indoor

Very Good	Good	Usable	Not Usable
weapons industry	furniture	musical instruments	construction wood
rotary cut veneer	parquet	staircases	plywood
	walls, decking		window frames
	paneling		laboratory furniture & fittings
	intarsia works		ship, rail & truck building
	cabinetmaking		blind veneer
	doors		
	flat sawn veneer		
	modeling		

BUMANI *(Schrebera arborea)*

Family: *Meliaceae*

Other Names: *mulere*
D.R. of the Congo: *bumani*

HABITAT
The little-known bumani tree species is found exclusively in the evergreen rain forests of the Eastern Congo basin, growing individually or in small groups. Some Congo residents refer to the tree as mulere.

TREE DESCRIPTION
This tree is 25–35 m (82–115 ft) tall and 60–90 cm (2–3 ft) in diameter. The trunk is straight and cylindrical, with up to 20 m (66 ft) of usable timber. Root buttresses extend from up to 2 m (6.5 ft) up the shaft.

WOOD DESCRIPTION
The sapwood and core wood are similar in appearance. The sapwood has a somewhat felt-like grain, while the core wood has an almost even, nonporous, ochre-colored structure. In electrical light it evidences a shiny glow, which becomes somewhat stronger after being dried; when the wood is used as ceiling paneling, artificial light can create a fascinating reflection on it.

Durability Class	IV	E – Module	9,800 N/mm^2
Raw density	0.58 g/cm^3	Volume dwindle	5.7 %
Bending strength	48 N/mm^2	Tangential shrinkage	-
Compression strength	-	Radial shrinkage	-

PROPERTIES AND APPLICATIONS

Bumani is a medium-hard wood; it is generally not difficult to work with, although drying should be carried out slowly. Since it quickly absorbs moisture, it should be chemically treated to provide a measure of water resistance. Bumani is only suitable for indoor purposes. It makes a beautiful veneer and is also used in the production of furniture panels, cabinetmaking, and modeling.

USES
Indoor

Very Good	Good	Usable	Not Usable
intarsia works	furniture	doors	construction wood
flat sawn veneer	walls, decking	weapons industry	flooring
	paneling	blind veneer	musical instruments
	cabinetmaking		plywood
	rotary cut veneer		staircases
	modeling		window frames
			laboratory furniture & fittings
			ship, rail & truck building

CEDAR, EAST AFRICAN *(Juniperus procera)*

Family: *Cupressaceae*

Other Names: *African pencil cedar*
Kenya: *Kenya cedar,*
                     East African juniper,
                     trakuet, tarakit
Ethiopia: *zahdi, cindira, thed*
Tanzania: *trakuet, tarakit*
Uganda: *mukuru, tolokyo*

HABITAT

This cedar species can be found in East Africa, with the largest concentration being in Tanzania. It grows in mountain regions up to 2,700 m (8,858 ft) in elevation.

TREE DESCRIPTION

This fast-growing tree is the largest cedar species in Africa, reaching heights of up to 45 m (148 ft). The trunk—often rather shapeless in appearance—has a diameter of 120–200 cm (4–6.5 ft), and the base frequently exhibits high, twisting roots. The core wood often suffers from decomposition (commonly called Red Core Decay).

WOOD DESCRIPTION:

East African cedar is nearly 50–70 percent whitish-yellow sapwood, which clearly contrasts with the yellow-red to reddish-brown core wood. The wood is somewhat heavier and harder than the American cedar *Juniperus virginiana*.

Durability Class	II	E – Module	11,400 N/mm²
Raw density	0.52 – 0.65 g/cm³	Volume dwindle	9.8 %
Bending strength	102 N/mm²	Tangential shrinkage	7.2 %
Compression strength	67 N/mm²	Radial shrinkage	5.7 %

PROPERTIES AND APPLICATIONS

This hard timber possesses good pressure and bending strengths, making it easy to work with. The drying process should be carried out in a slow and careful manner; kiln drying will stop any decomposition that might be occurring. Cedar, being durable and weather resistant, has a wide variety of applications. It is used in the production of parquet, panels, pencils, fences, cabinets, and for siding and roof shingles in home construction.

USES
Indoor/Outdoor

Very Good	Good	Usable	Not Usable
paneling	construction wood	intarsia works	
	furniture	musical instruments	
	flooring	plywood	
	walls, decking	laboratory furniture & fittings	
	cabinetmaking	weapons industry	
	doors	rotary cut veneer	
	staircases	flat sawn veneer	
	window frames		
	ship, rail & truck building		
	blind veneer		
	modeling		

CORDIA *(Cordia abyssenica)*

Family:	*Boraginaceae*

Other Names:
Sudan: *Sudan teak*
Nigeria: *omo, aiiba*
Cameroon: *ebais, ebe*
Rep. of the Congo: *sumba*
D.R. of the Congo: *mfutu, mugona*
Kenya: *samut, ahui*

HABITAT
Cordia grows exclusively in Ethiopia, Kenya, Uganda, and the eastern part of the Democratic Republic of the Congo. The tree thrives in the warm and humid climatic conditions of the subtropical rain forests found in this region's mountains and typically grows at elevations between 1,200–1,800 m (3,937–5,906 ft).

TREE DESCRIPTION
Cordia trees are between 25–30 m (82–98 ft) tall with diameters of 70–180 cm (2.5–6 ft). The species' trunk, which carries a large crown, has a mostly crooked and irregular structure; limbs appear at fairly low positions, resulting in rather small timber lengths. Large elderly trees are invariably rotten at the core.

WOOD DESCRIPTION
The yellowish sapwood can be up to 6 cm (2.4 in) thick. The core wood has a twisting or interlocked grain and is generally light- or pinkish-brown, often with a sheen. After cutting, the wood will take on a bluish hue if not properly dried and fumigated. Otherwise, many pleasing variations in appearance (some intensely colorful) may result, such as gold-brown, violet-yellow and yellow-brown with dark stripes.

Durability Class	III	**E – Module**	-
Raw density	0.41 g/cm³	**Volume dwindle**	8.1 %
Bending strength	65 N/mm²	**Tangential shrinkage**	4.8 %
Compression strength	8.1 – 28 N/mm²	**Radial shrinkage**	3.6 %

PROPERTIES AND APPLICATIONS

Cordia is, despite its low weight, a dense and solid wood. However, its mechanical properties are mediocre. It is primarily a decorative, walnut-like tree useful for purposes such as interior finish work and furniture veneers. It also has many applications in the manufacture of musical instruments, and German wood turners enjoy using this wood for artistic works. The timber is sufficiently weather resistant for use in exterior projects such as panels and balconies.

USES

Indoor/Outdoor

Very Good	Good	Usable	Not Usable
	furniture	construction wood	plywood
	flooring	staircases	laboratory furniture & fittings
	walls, decking	window frames	ship, rail & truck building
	paneling	blind veneer	weapons industry
	intarsia works		modeling
	musical instruments		
	cabinetmaking		
	doors		
	rotary cut veneer		
	flat sawn veneer		

COULA *(Coula edulis)*

Family:	*Olacaceae*
Other Names:	*almond wood*
Liberia:	*Liberian walnut, srah*
Ivory Coast:	*attia, petembe*
Nigeria:	*nkula, omumu*
Cameroon:	*woulu, ewome*
Rep. of the Congo:	*kumumu, efombe*
Gabon:	*ogoula, ehoumer, skoumbi*

HABITAT

Coula can be found growing in groups in evergreen rain forests and among deciduous trees in mixed damp forests. Its range extends from Liberia to the Republic of the Congo.

TREE DESCRIPTION

This medium-sized tree can reach heights of up to 40 m (131 ft), with diameters ranging from 60–100 cm (2–3.5 ft). The trunk is cylindrical and clear of branches for up to 20 m (66 ft). Coula fruit is similar to that of walnut.

WOOD DESCRIPTION

The thin sapwood is white in color, whereas the core wood is pinkish- to reddish-brown with wavy stripes. The fibers are very fine, giving a firm, even quality to the wood.

Durability Class	II	**E – Module**	13,700 N/mm²
Raw density	0.80 g/cm³	**Volume dwindle**	15.4 %
Bending strength	140 N/mm²	**Tangential shrinkage**	9.2 %
Compression strength	80 N/mm²	**Radial shrinkage**	5.1 %

PROPERTIES AND APPLICATIONS

Coula is durable with good mechanical properties. It dries without much difficulty, although a constant temperature must be applied when kiln drying to prevent tears in the wood. Coula is commonly used for parquet, windows, doors and panels, and as a substitute for iroko and afrormosia. Its durability and weather resistance allow it to be used for exterior building timber.

USES

Indoor/Outdoor

Very Good	Good	Usable	Not Usable
	construction wood	intarsia works	musical instruments
	furniture	cabinetmaking	plywood
	flooring	laboratory furniture & fittings	
	walls, decking	weapons industry	
	paneling	rotary cut veneer	
	doors	modeling	
	staircases		
	window frames		
	ship, rail & truck building		
	flat sawn veneer		
	blind veneer		

DABEMA *(Piptadeniastrum africanum)*

Family:	*Mimosaceae*

Other Names:
Ghana:	*dahoma*
Nigeria:	*agboin, ekhimi*
Cameroon:	*atui, bokombolo*
D.R. of the Congo:	*banzu, bokundu, singa*
Germany:	*African oak*

HABITAT

Dabema is primarily found in deciduous rain forests; its range extends throughout much of tropical Africa, from Senegal in the west to Sudan and Uganda in the east.

TREE DESCRIPTION

Dabema is an imposing tree with an umbrella-like crown. It grows to approximately 40 m (131 ft) in height, with an average trunk diameter of 60–120 cm (2–4 ft). The lower trunk has high and prominent root buttresses which minimize timber output; the straight and cylindrical section of the bole above the roots is no longer than 15 m (49 ft). Segments of the trunk may exhibit twisted growth.

WOOD DESCRIPTION

The sapwood is about 5 cm (2 in) thick. Its white-gray or light-brown coloration demarcates it from the core wood, whose color varies between gray-brown and pale golden-brown (frequently with a green or golden luster). Dabema has a coarse texture and an interlocked grain pattern.

Durability Class	II	**E – Module**	13,000 N/mm²
Raw density	0.70 g/cm³	**Volume dwindle**	12.4 %
Bending strength	110 N/mm²	**Tangential shrinkage**	8.5 %
Compression strength	58 N/mm²	**Radial shrinkage**	4.2 %

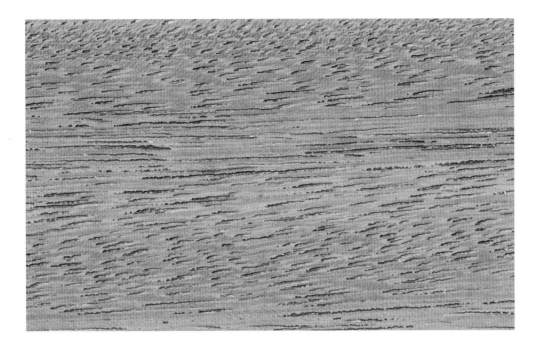

PROPERTIES AND APPLICATIONS

Dabema is a solid, medium-hard wood that can serve as an excellent general replacement for oak. It is well-suited for solid-wood uses such as bridge and building construction. Dabema is easily peeled after being well-steamed, making is useful for processing as plywood. Boards should be treated with undiluted oxalic acid, since a strong ammonia smell emanates from this wood.

USES
Indoor/Outdoor

Very Good	Good	Usable	Not Usable	
construction wood	plywood		furniture	flat sawn veneer
ship, rail &			flooring	blind veneer
truck building			walls, decking	modeling
			paneling	rotary cut veneer
			intarsia works	
			musical instruments	
			cabinetmaking	
			doors	
			staircases	
			window frames	
			laboratory furniture & fittings	
			weapons industry	

DIBETOU *(Lovoa trichilioides)*

Family: *Meliaceae*

Other Names: *African walnut*
Cameroon: *bibolo, apopo, lavoa*
Gabon: *bibolo, sida*
Ghana: *penkwa*
Congo countries: *lifaki, muindu*

HABITAT
Dibetou's habitat extends from the lower rain forests of Sierra Leone in the west to the Congo region in the east. It is most frequently found scattered about in areas subject to heavy rainfall.

TREE DESCRIPTION
This large, broad-leafed evergreen can grow to 50 m (164 ft) in height. The trunk tends to be straight with little tapering; its standard diameter is 60–90 cm (2–3 ft), while its maximum diameter is about 120 cm (4 ft). Approximately 25 m (82 ft) is free of branches. Dibetou characteristically has root buttresses forming at a height of about 2 m (6.5 ft).

WOOD DESCRIPTION
The sapwood is slim (no more than 5 cm (2 in) thick) and grayish-white to brownish-yellow in color. The clearly differentiated core wood is pale walnut-brown, often with a red or gold-brown glint; it eventually darkens if exposed to light. The wood is generally veined with glossy stripes.

Durability Class	II	E – Module	8,400 N/mm^2
Raw density	0.53 – 0.63 g/cm^3	Volume dwindle	9.3 %
Bending strength	82 N/mm^2	Tangential shrinkage	5.5 %
Compression strength	52 N/mm^2	Radial shrinkage	3.6 %

PROPERTIES AND APPLICATIONS

Dibetou has a high bending strength and can be easily processed to manufacture rotary-cut veneers. After the pores are properly filled, the wood can be polished, varnished, painted and glued without difficulty. Its good physical properties make it suitable for decorative furniture carpentry, particularly for antique furniture, chairs and upholstered furniture. It is also used for gunstocks.

USES

Indoor

Very Good	Good	Usable	Not Usable
furniture	walls, decking	flooring	construction wood
weapons industry	paneling	cabinetmaking	musical instruments
rotary cut veneer	intarsia works		plywood
	doors		window frames
	staircases		laboratory furniture & fittings
	flat sawn veneer		ship, rail & truck building
			blind veneer
			modeling

DIFOU *(Morus mesozygia)*

Family: *Moraceae*

Other Names:
Mozambique: *mecodze, turero*
D.R. of the Congo: *kankate, okwandia*
Uganda: *kivulevule*
Tanzania: *mukimbi*

HABITAT
Difou, found mainly in Mozambique and the Democratic Republic of the Congo, favors semi-humid transitional regions.

TREE DESCRIPTION
This small tree has a maximum height of 30 m (98 ft). The mostly straight-growing trunk, which is 50–80 cm (1.5–2.5 ft) in diameter, is just half of the total height of the tree. Much potentially usable timber is compromised because of the extensive root system growing out of the base of the bole.

WOOD DESCRIPTION
Freshly-felled difou core wood possesses a luminous yellow color, quite different from the almost white sapwood. The core wood soon darkens to a gold- to reddish-brown hue, similar to iroko.

Durability Class	II	**E – Module**	16,000 N/mm²
Raw density	0.77 – 0.90 g/cm³	**Volume dwindle**	7.8 – 11.0 %
Bending strength	164 N/mm²	**Tangential shrinkage**	5.6 %
Compression strength	88 N/mm²	**Radial shrinkage**	3.3 %

PROPERTIES AND APPLICATIONS

Correctly air-dried difou rarely experiences cracking or buckling, although the timber's susceptibility to attack by various fungi and insects makes chemical treatment advisable. Despite its frequently twisted growth, the wood can be easily worked with and is quite accommodating to the usual types of wood connections—glue, nails, bolts, etc. Difou is weather-sensitive and is therefore most appropriately used for interior projects. Its most common use is as a veneer, or for decorative and intarsia work.

USES

Indoor

Very Good	Good	Usable	Not Usable	
	rotary cut veneer	furniture	construction wood	ship, rail &
	flat swan veneer	paneling	flooring	truck building
		intarsia works	walls, decking	weapons industry
			musical instruments	blind veneer
			cabinetmaking	modeling
			plywood	
			doors	
			staircases	
			window frames	
			laboratory furniture & fittings	

DOUSSIE / AFZELIA *(Afzelia africana)*

Family: *Caesalpiniaceae*

Other Names: *apa*
Cameroon: *doussie*
Ivory Coast: *lingue*
Ghana: *papao*
Congo countries: *bolengu, sifu sifu*
Angola: *uvala*
Tanzania: *mambakofi*

HABITAT
Doussie occupies a vast territory spanning much of the continent, from Senegal in West Africa to Mozambique in East Africa. The trees are scattered throughout the evergreen rain forests and the junction regions of the damp savannah. In Asia, afzelia is known as merbau and makamong.

TREE DESCRIPTION
The species can grow to 30–40 m (98–131 ft) in height and has a diameter of 80–120 cm (2.5–4 ft). The trunk is often filled with dents; it tends to grow in an even, cylindrical manner, and may be clear of branches for up to 20 m (66 ft). The roots are rarely visible above ground.

WOOD DESCRIPTION
There are two varieties of this species, commonly referred to as doussie rouge and doussie blanc. These share the same habitat, but the first is qualitatively and technologically superior to the second. Both types have a very even wood fiber and a thin, clearly differentiated band of white-gray sapwood. The core woods differ in color, as their names imply, and typically darken upon exposure to light and air, although occasionally a light pink color is the end result.

Durability Class	II	E – Module	14,500 N/mm²
Raw density	0.75 g/cm³	Volume dwindle	7.0 %
Bending strength	117 N/mm²	Tangential shrinkage	4.0 %
Compression strength	69 N/mm²	Radial shrinkage	2.6 %

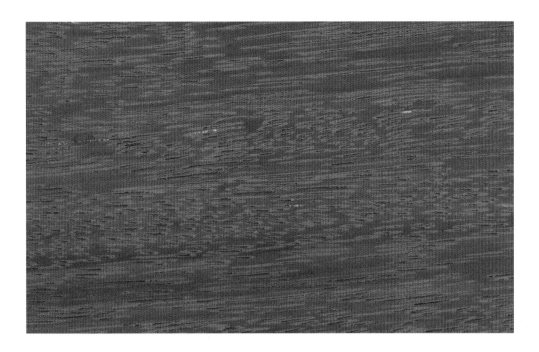

PROPERTIES AND APPLICATIONS

Doussie is a hard and heavy wood, comparable to iroko, and having similar uses. It is very stable and fairly flexible. Kiln drying must be performed continuously and slowly; the wood's small shrinkage property results in no cracking during drying. Doussie is an excellent choice for solid-wood furniture, parquet, heavy-duty flooring, laboratory furniture, school benches and garden furniture. Oil-based paint adheres badly to the wood, but clear lacquers and polyurethane have been successfully applied by European woodworkers.

USES

Indoor/Outdoor

Very Good	Good	Usable	Not Usable
construction wood	furniture	paneling	intarsia works
flooring	walls, decking	cabinetmaking	musical instruments
laboratory furniture & fittings	doors	weapons industry	plywood
ship, rail & truck building	staircases	modeling	blind veneer
	window frames		
	rotary cut veneer		
	flat sawn veneer		

EBONY / EBENE D'AFRIQUE *(Diospyros crassiflora)*

Family:	*Ebenaceae*

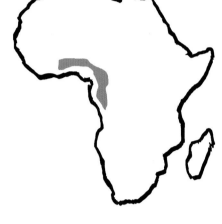

Other Names:	*maba*
Nigeria:	*old calabar, kanrou*
Cameroon:	*ebony, ebenier, n'dou*
Spain:	*ebano*
Portugal:	*ebano*
Ghana:	*omenova*

HABITAT
The rare ebony (or ebene) tree can be found in various countries bordering the Gulf of Guinea; the species particularly flourishes in Nigeria, Cameroon and Gabon, with some varieties growing best in evergreen rain forests. Related species grow in niches in East African countries such as Madagascar, Mauritius and Tanzania. Although the ebony tree family is common worldwide, the African varieties are particularly expensive and valuable.

TREE DESCRIPTION
The tree is small in stature, with a maximum height of approximately 20 m (66 ft) and a diameter between 40–70 cm (1.5–2.5 ft). The trunk is cylindrical and free of branches, at most 6 m (20 ft) in height, and has no above-ground rootage.

WOOD DESCRIPTION
The sapwood is reddish-gray to grayish-brown, occasionally yellowish, and is basically useless. The valuable heartwood may be gray-brown, black-brown, greenish or jet black in color, depending upon the specific region the tree is growing in. The proportion of core wood in this tree is usually very high. White-scored marks in the heartwood often indicate a wood defect and thus inferior quality.

Durability Class	I	E – Module	12,900 N/mm^2
Raw density	1.0 – 1.2 g/cm^3	Volume dwindle	21.0 %
Bending strength	140 N/mm^2	Tangential shrinkage	12.8 %
Compression strength	57 N/mm^2	Radial shrinkage	8.2 %

PROPERTIES AND APPLICATIONS

Ebony is one of the heaviest woods in the world, and its extreme compression and bending strengths are almost metallic in nature—all of which make the wood very difficult to cut. In small quantities the wood dries quickly, although sections with larger diameters are inclined to crack. Ebony is quite weather- and insect-resistant. It is used extensively in the production of expensive veneers, musical instruments (flutes, piano keys), mathematical instruments, chess pieces, and various other luxury articles. By convention, ebony is divided by quality into three classes: 1) black ebony (the highest class) possesses homogenous, pure black coloring; 2) king ebony is black with dark red stripes; 3) queen ebony (the lowest class) is black with irregular yellow or orange stripes.

USES
Indoor/Outdoor

Very Good	Good	Usable	Not Usable
furniture	flooring	construction wood	plywood
intarsia works	walls, decking	doors	staircases
musical instruments	paneling		window frames
cabinetmaking	laboratory furniture		ship, rail & truck building
weapons industry	& fittings		blind veneer
rotary cut veneer			
flat sawn veneer			
modeling			

55

EFFEU *(Hannoa klaineana)*

Family: *Simaroubaceae*

Other Names:
Liberia: *yaglü, zauh*
Ivory Coast: *apohia*
Ghana: *feutia*
Nigeria: *igbo*
Cameroon: *nom ozek*
Congo countries: *babolo*

HABITAT
Effeu's preferred habitat is humid evergreen forests. The tree can be found throughout much of West and Central Africa, from Sierra Leone to Angola and deep into the Congo basin.

TREE DESCRIPTION
Effeu trees are distinguished by their straight, slim, cylindrical trunks. They reach heights of 30–35 m (98–115 ft) and have diameters of 80–120 cm (2.5–4 ft). There is no root buttressing; the crown begins at about 24 m (79 ft) above the ground.

WOOD DESCRIPTION
The sapwood and core wood are both yellowish-white. The core wood is very soft with straight fibers.

Durability Class	IV	E – Module	8,200 N/mm²
Raw density	0.33 – 0.45 g/cm³	Volume dwindle	10.0 – 11.0 %
Bending strength	53 N/mm²	Tangential shrinkage	6.0 %
Compression strength	22 N/mm²	Radial shrinkage	3.3 %

PROPERTIES AND APPLICATIONS

The timber is light and not very solid and is therefore quite workable. Its raw density and strength values are not very high. The wood peels easily, and its porous surface nicely absorbs common treatments. Effeu is mainly used for indoor applications or for the production of shipping crates to transport breakable or easily bruised items such as small machinery and fruit.

USES

Indoor

Very Good	Good	Usable	Not Usable
	plywood	rotary cut veneer	construction wood
	flat sawn veneer		furniture
	blind veneer		flooring
	modeling		walls, decking
			paneling
			intarsia works
			musical instruments
			cabinetmaking
			doors
			staircases
			window frames
			laboratory furniture & fittings
			ship, rail & truck building
			weapons industry

EKABA *(Tetraberlinia bifoliolata)*

Family: *Caesalpiniaceae*

Other Names: *ekop*
Cameroon: *ribi, ekop ribi*
Equatorial-Guinea: *akaba*
Gabon: *eko, ekaba*
Congo countries: *mudunghu*

HABITAT
Ekaba is a rare species found growing in small groups. Its territory extends from southern Cameroon to the northern boundary of Angola, and from the Atlantic Ocean to the western regions of the Democratic Republic of the Congo.

TREE DESCRIPTION
The ekaba is a large tree with a height of between 30–45 m (98–148 ft) and a diameter of up to 100 cm (3.5 ft). The trunk is straight and cylindrical with little above-ground rootage. The bark of freshly cut ekaba wood can be wiped off the trunk with a cloth.

WOOD DESCRIPTION
The yellowish- to grayish-white sapwood is approximately 10 cm (3.9 in) thick and not very differentiated from the core wood, which after cutting, discolors to a pinkish-copper color. Dark lines between 9–15 mm (.4–.6 in) long are typically present, and calcium oxalate may be stored in the pores.

Durability Class	III	E – Module	9,400 N/mm²
Raw density	0.60 g/cm³	Volume dwindle	13.5 %
Bending strength	80 N/mm²	Tangential shrinkage	8.0 %
Compression strength	40 N/mm²	Radial shrinkage	4.0 %

PROPERTIES AND APPLICATIONS

This hard and moderately strong wood has reasonably good physical properties, including an above average elasticity. It dries slowly—occasionally with deformations—and is not particularly weather- or insect-resistant. Ekaba is used in the plywood industry and in the production of veneers.

USES

Indoor

Very Good	Good	Usable	Not Usable
	plywood	furniture	construction wood
	rotary cut veneer	flooring	musical instruments
	flat sawn veneer	walls, decking	doors
	blind veneer	paneling	staircases
	modeling	intarsia works	window frames
		cabinetmaking	laboratory furniture & fittings
			ship, rail & truck building
			weapons industry

EMIEN *(Alstonia congensis)*

Family:	*Apocynaceae*	

Other Names:

Congo countries:	*tsonguti, akuka, ubangi, moguga*
Sierra Leone:	*kaiwi*
Ivory Coast:	*onguie*
Cameroon:	*ekouk, kanja*
Uganda:	*mujua*
Tanzania:	*mujwa*
Angola:	*nfomba*
Gabon:	*kuge, kaika*

HABITAT

Emien is a broad-leafed tree of the tropical evergreen forest. It inhabits a broad swath of Africa, stretching along the Atlantic from Sierra Leone to Angola, and deep into the Congo basin. Emien also grows in Asia.

TREE DESCRIPTION

This large, quick-growing tree often reaches heights of more than 36 m (118 ft), with diameters ranging from 60–80 cm (2–2.5 ft). A distinguishing characteristic are its high, slim root buttresses, which can be found growing up to 6 m (20 ft) up the base of the trunk. The trunk is largely cylindrical and may have patches of softer, less dense wood; it is clear of branches for about 20 m (66 ft). Locals use the bark for medicinal purposes.

WOOD DESCRIPTION

Both core wood and sapwood are pale yellow but darken appreciably upon exposure to air; the sapwood zone is frequently over 15 cm (5.9 in) thick. Growth rings are differentiated by the different coloring of more recent wood. A distinguishing characteristic is the latex excretions which create light colored stripes of up to 20 mm (.8 in) in radial length.

Durability Class	III	**E – Module**	7,500 N/mm^2
Raw density	0.43 g/cm^3	**Volume dwindle**	9.3 %
Bending strength	52 N/mm^2	**Tangential shrinkage**	5.3 %
Compression strength	27 N/mm^2	**Radial shrinkage**	3.8 %

PROPERTIES AND APPLICATIONS

Emien is a light, soft, medium-fine wood with straight fibers. As a result, the wood is not very pliable and has a low dynamic strength. Warping occurs only rarely with drying. Emien's homogeneous fiber structure makes the wood suitable for the manufacture of veneers, plywood and carpenter plates. The wood is additionally used in the production of furniture and musical instruments, as well as for carving projects and modeling work. It is also converted to wood wool (excelsior) used in packing boxes for tropical fruit.

USES
Indoor

Very Good	Good	Usable	Not Usable
	furniture	intarsia works	construction wood
	plywood	musical instruments	flooring
	rotary cut veneer	cabinetmaking	walls, decking
	flat sawn veneer		paneling
	blind veneer		doors
	modeling		staircases
			window frames
			laboratory furniture & fittings
			ship, rail & truck building
			weapons industry

ESSESSANG *(Ricinodendron heudelotii)*

Family: *Euphorbiaceae*

Other Names:

United Kingdom:	*erimado*
France:	*essessang*
D.R. of the Congo:	*mulela, sanga sanga*
Sierra Leone:	*gholei, ekok*
Ivory Coast:	*kotoue, poposi*
Ghana:	*awuma, epuwi, wama*
Nigeria:	*potopoto, ekku*
Cameroon:	*ehan, esango*

HABITAT

Essessang is common in tropical West and Central Africa. It is a quick growing tree, favoring mountainside zones of elevations up to 1,300 m (4,265 ft) above sea level.

TREE DESCRIPTION

The species can be up to 40 m (131 ft) tall, with a diameter of 80–150 cm (2.5–5 ft). The trunks are typically slim and straight growing; the branch-free section suitable as timber is a maximum of 25 m (82 ft) in length. The trunk base may have small root buttresses.

WOOD DESCRIPTION

The bark is reddish-white; both core wood and sapwood are a pale yellow straw-like color and indistinguishable from each other. Sometimes the wood color is affected by fungus. Pore density and size can vary markedly between growth rings.

Durability Class	V	**E – Module**	4,800 N/mm²
Raw density	0.26 – 0.30 g/cm³	**Volume dwindle**	9.6 %
Bending strength	40 N/mm²	**Tangential shrinkage**	5.0 %
Compression strength	21 N/mm²	**Radial shrinkage**	-

PROPERTIES AND APPLICATIONS

The porous wood consists of fine, straight fibers, and possesses strength properties comparable with those of balsa wood. Essessang dries quickly (but has a slight tendency toward deformation) and is very sensitive to insect and fungus attacks. The wood's weaknesses restrict its usefulness, so its primary application is as an interior veneer layer in plywood. It is also used as a cork substitute for flotation products.

USES
Indoor

Very Good	Good	Usable	Not Usable
modeling	blind veneer	furniture	construction wood
		intarsia works	flooring
		plywood	walls, decking
		laboratory furniture & fittings	paneling
		rotary cut veneer	musical instruments
		flat sawn veneer	cabinetmaking
			doors
			staircases
			window frames
			ship, rail & truck building
			weapons industry

ESSIA *(Petersianthus macrocarpus)*

Family: *Lecythidaceae*

Other Names:
Ivory Coast: *abale*
Ghana: *esia, osa*
Nigeria: *stinkwood, owewe*
Cameroon: *abing*
D.R. of the Congo: *bosaki, wulo, minzu*

HABITAT
Essia is widely distributed throughout West and Central Africa. It inhabits both humid rain forests and, less frequently, dry zones.

TREE DESCRIPTION
Essia can grow to heights of more than 40 m (131 ft), with diameters of up to 120 cm (4 ft). The trunk is cylindrical and straight, with a shaft of 15–20 m (49–66 ft) suitable for timber; the base lacks root buttresses but is naturally thick and irregular.

WOOD DESCRIPTION
The pale yellow-white sapwood is up to 10 cm (3.9 in) thick and differentiated from the pinkish-brown core wood. The core wood is veined with dark stripes which give the wood a stained and decorative appearance.

Durability Class	II	E – Module	12,100 N/mm^2
Raw density	0.73 g/cm^3	Volume dwindle	14.8 – 23.8 %
Bending strength	132 N/mm^2	Tangential shrinkage	9.2 %
Compression strength	60 N/mm^2	Radial shrinkage	5.7 %

PROPERTIES AND APPLICATIONS

Essia is quite hard and heavy and possesses good mechanical and dynamic properties. Natural drying must be done with care as that process tends to crack and deform the wood. Essia is used as a general construction wood and for laboratory furnishings. It has also been used recently in Europe to make both rotary cut and flat sawn veneers. With proper drying, this beautiful, decoratively striped wood can be a good choice for furniture manufacturing.

USES

Indoor/Outdoor

Very Good	Good	Usable	Not Usable
	construction wood	paneling	musical instruments
	furniture	intarsia works	cabinetmaking
	flooring	ship, rail & truck building	plywood
	walls, decking	weapons industry	staircases
	doors		window frames
	laboratory furniture & fittings		blind veneer
	rotary cut veneer		modeling
	flat sawn veneer		

EYONG *(Sterculia tragacantha) or (Eribroma oblonga)*

Family: *Sterculiaceae*

Other Names:
Ivory Coast: *bi, azodo, assasodou*
Nigeria: *okoko, orodo, ebenebe*
Cameroon: *bongele, dototo, lom*
D.R. of the Congo: *bongo, moan*

HABITAT

Eyong is a typical representative of trees of the transitional zone from the rain forest to the dry savannah (where it is most frequently found). It is primarily a coastal species whose habitat extends from Liberia to Angola; it is sometimes also found in the inner Congo basin.

TREE DESCRIPTION

This deciduous tree has a height of 35 m (115 ft) and a diameter of up to 80 cm (2.5 ft). The smooth, cylindrical trunk can reach a height of up to 25 m (82 ft) before branches appear; the base manifests narrow, wing-like root buttresses, some up to 4 m (13 ft) high. A total length of some 15–20 m (49–66 ft) is usable as timber. These trees should be felled after their leaf-shedding cycle is over.

WOOD DESCRIPTION

Eyong has a thick—up to 20 cm (7.9 in)—yellowish-white sapwood. The somewhat darker core wood can be pale yellow to yellowish-brown in color. The structure of the wood is moderately hard, medium-heavy and coarse. The irregularly scattered pores are rough and not very numerous.

Durability Class	III	E – Module	13,600 N/mm²
Raw density	0.70 – 0.80 g/cm³	Volume dwindle	16.6 %
Bending strength	110 N/mm²	Tangential shrinkage	12.0 %
Compression strength	50 N/mm²	Radial shrinkage	4.8 %

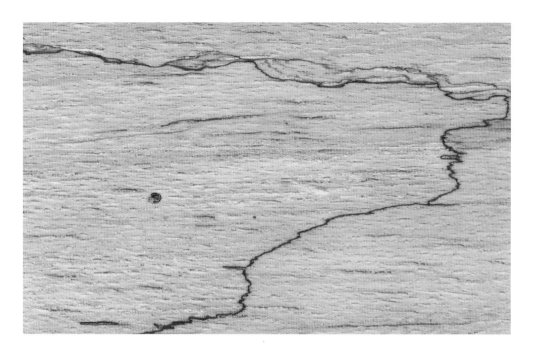

PROPERTIES AND APPLICATIONS

Because of eyong's propensity to shrink, drying must be carefully carried out. Appropriate steam and hot water treatments can effectively combat the timber's tendency to crack. From a mechanical perspective, eyong is solid, flexible and pliable. It is a popular choice for solid wood furniture manufacturing and for plywood. Tests in Spain have shown that eyong is especially suitable for fire protection doors.

USES
Indoor/Outdoor

Very Good	Good	Usable	Not Usable
plywood	furniture		construction wood
blind veneer	doors		flooring
	modeling		walls, decking
			paneling
			intarsia works
			musical instruments
			cabinetmaking
			staircases
			window frames
			laboratory furniture & fittings
			ship, rail & truck building
			weapons industry
			rotary cut veneer
			flat sawn veneer

FRAMIRE *(Terminalia ivorensis)*

Family: *Combretaceae*

Other Names: *frake, limbo*
Liberia: *deohr, bajii, bassi*
Ivory Coast: *agru, bona, cauri*
Nigeria: *afara, idigbo, treme*
Cameroon: *lidia*
Rep. of the Congo: *limbo*
Ghana: *emri, idigbo*

HABITAT
Framire, from the limba family, grows in evergreen rain forests and damp savannah regions. Its range of distribution is from Sierra Leone in the west to the Democratic Republic of the Congo in the east; particularly large clusters of the tree can be found in Ivory Coast.

TREE DESCRIPTION
Framire is a straight-growing tree that can reach heights of up to 50 m (164 ft) and diameters of 60–100 cm (2–3.5 ft). Up to 30 m (98 ft) of the trunk is clear of branches. Older trunks may have rot in the core wood.

WOOD DESCRIPTION
The sapwood is yellow, the core wood yellow-green. After being sawn, the wood takes on a yellowish- or pinkish-brown coloration. The pores are irregularly patterned, appearing either individually or in scattered pairs. This structural property makes the wood a frequent choice for use in veneers.

Durability Class	III		**E – Module**	11,300 N/mm²
Raw density	0.50 – 0.60 g/cm³		**Volume dwindle**	9.9 %
Bending strength	84 N/mm²		**Tangential shrinkage**	5.5 %
Compression strength	45 N/mm²		**Radial shrinkage**	3.7 %

PROPERTIES AND APPLICATIONS

Framire has approximately the same hardness, specific weight and physical properties as oak. The drying process is typically trouble-free. The wood is ideal for receiving applications of lacquers, glazes or liquid waxes; however, direct contact with metal should be avoided to prevent the transfer of corrosion marks onto the wood. Framire is a beautiful veneer wood and can be used for both interior and exterior applications. It is also utilized by the musical instrument industry, particularly in the production of string instruments.

USES
Indoor/Outdoor

Very Good	Good	Usable	Not Usable
musical instruments	construction wood	intarsia works	
window frames	furniture	plywood	
	flooring	laboratory furniture & fittings	
	walls, decking	weapons industry	
	paneling		
	cabinetmaking		
	doors		
	staircases		
	ship, rail & truck building		
	rotary cut veneer		
	flat sawn veneer		
	blind veneer		
	modeling		

FUMA *(Ceiba pentandra)*

Family:	*Bombacaceae*
Other Names:	*cottonwood, formager, ceiba*
Ivory Coast:	*enia*
Nigeria:	*okha*
Cameroon:	*doum*
Congo countries:	*buleda*

HABITAT
Fuma occupies a vast habitat in Africa, its range extending from the Atlantic to the Indian Ocean. The species is also resident in tropical and subtropical South America, West India, Sri Lanka, the Philippines and tropical regions of Australia. It is found in both evergreen rain forests and deciduous forests.

TREE DESCRIPTION
Fuma is a tall, quick-growing tree, reaching heights of up to 50 m (164 ft). The trunk, which is straight and cylindrical, has a diameter ranging from 100–250 cm (3.5–8 ft), with few if any branches appearing lower than 20 m (66 ft) above the ground.

WOOD DESCRIPTION
Fuma wood is usually gray to yellowish-white, with common variations being a partial pinkish or brownish coloration. The heartwood and sapwood rarely contrast in appearance. The wood's fiber structure is straight and regular.

Durability Class	IV	E – Module	4,100 N/mm^2
Raw density	0.30 – 0.40 g/cm^3	Volume dwindle	11.0 %
Bending strength	41 N/mm^2	Tangential shrinkage	6.7 %
Compression strength	21 N/mm^2	Radial shrinkage	3.0 %

PROPERTIES AND APPLICATIONS

Although a pliable, lighter wood, Fuma possesses a fair compression strength and is sufficiently tough. It is responsive to gluing and is therefore suitable for the production of blind veneers and plywood. Because of its low weight, it is also used in the manufacture of wooden sandals, light containers, models, and heels for ladies' shoes. Finally, as the wood has a beautiful structure, it can produce rotary cut veneers or high-quality decorative panels for such things as walls and furniture.

USES

Indoor

Very Good	Good	Usable	Not Usable
	plywood	walls, decking	construction wood
	flat sawn veneer	rotary cut veneer	furniture
	blind veneer		flooring
	modeling		paneling
			intarsia works
			musical instruments
			cabinetmaking
			doors
			staircases
			window frames
			laboratory furniture & fittings
			ship, rail & truck building
			weapons industry

GRENADILL *(Dalbergia melanoxylon)*

Family:	*Papilionaceae*
Other Names:	*African blackwood*
Mozambique:	*pau preto,*
	ebene Mozambique
Uganda:	*mufunjo*
Senegal:	*palissandre de Senegal*
Togo:	*atiyi*
Cameroon:	*epindepinde*
Tanzania:	*mpingo*

HABITAT

The grenadill tree (also commonly known as the African blackwood) belongs to the palissandre family. Most other *Dalbergia* varieties grow in Brazil and are referred to as palissandre-jacaranda or cocobolo. In international trading, a distinction must be made between African blackwood, the genuine American grenadill (*Brya ebenus*), and Australian blackwood (*Acacia melanoxylon*).

TREE DESCRIPTION

Grenadill is a small tree, often little more than a bush, with a height of 10 m (33 ft) and a diameter of 40–60 cm (1.5–2 ft). Due to its small stature and bent shape, the amount of usable wood is only about 3 m (10 ft) in length. Additionally, older trunks are often hollow inside.

WOOD DESCRIPTION

The sapwood is a maximum of 20 mm (.8 in) deep and whitish-brown in color; the core wood is brown to black violet. The wood emits a tar-like odor when burned. Grenadill is one of the most expensive available timbers; it resembles ebony (*Diospyros crassiflora*) and is sometimes falsely advertised as such.

Durability Class	I	E – Module	16,000 N/mm²
Raw density	1.25 g/cm³	Volume dwindle	15.0 %
Bending strength	170 N/mm²	Tangential shrinkage	5.0 %
Compression strength	90 N/mm²	Radial shrinkage	3.0 %

PROPERTIES AND APPLICATIONS

This firm, heavy wood possesses good flexibility characteristics. It is both water- and weather-resistant and dries slowly. It is a very hard timber that must be handled carefully and processed only with especially strong cutting equipment tools. Grenadill is a decorative wood that can be nicely polished. Common applications include the production of musical instruments (flutes and their mouthpieces, piano keys), mathematical instruments, chessmen or game pieces, and various other luxury items.

USES
Indoor/Outdoor

Very Good	Good	Usable	Not Usable
furniture	flooring	construction wood	plywood
intarsia works	walls, decking	doors	staircases
musical instruments	paneling	laboratory furniture & fittings	window frames
cabinetmaking	weapons industry		ship, rail & truck building
rotary cut veneer	modeling		blind veneer
flat sawn veneer			

IATANDZA *(Albizzia ferruginea)*

Family:	*Mimosaceae*

Other Names:	*musase*
Ivory Coast:	*yatandza*
Ghana:	*awiemfosamina*
D.R. of the Congo:	*elongwamba*
Cameroon:	*evouvous, ongo ayem*
Rep. of the Congo:	*sifou-sifou*

HABITAT

Iatandza grows throughout tropical Africa, from Sierra Leone in the northwest across Central Africa down to Zimbabwe in the southeast. It is found in both evergreen and deciduous forests; however, only some five or so mature specimens are likely to be found per acre.

TREE DESCRIPTION

This slim tree reaches a height of 35 m (115 ft), with trunk diameters varying between 60–120 cm (2–4 ft); the branchless span of trunk suitable for timber can measure up to 30 m (98 ft) in length. Some specimens have a rather misshapen, shrub-like appearance with low-hanging branches.

WOOD DESCRIPTION

The sapwood—approximately 7 cm (2.8 in) thick—is straw-colored, whereas the core wood is dark to reddish-brown (and sometimes partially violet-colored). Iatandza, which is anatomically similar to the closely related Asian kokko, is a hard wood with a rough structure.

Durability Class	II	**E – Module**	10,000 N/mm^2
Raw density	0.60 g/cm^3	**Volume dwindle**	9.4 %
Bending strength	95 N/mm^2	**Tangential shrinkage**	5.2 %
Compression strength	50 N/mm^2	**Radial shrinkage**	3.0%

PROPERTIES AND APPLICATIONS

Iatandza possesses good strength properties and is rarely subject to insect attack. Because of its favorable technological characteristics, it is widely used for interior construction (beams, decking, etc.), although it is not sufficiently durable for exterior purposes. Iatandza is commonly used in furniture production, woodturning, and for interior work. If stripped, samples of sufficient quality may be suitable for veneer production.

USES
Indoor

Very Good	Good	Usable	Not Usable
paneling	construction wood	window frames	intarsia works
doors	furniture	laboratory furniture & fittings	plywood
flat sawn veneer	flooring	weapons industry	ship, rail & truck building
	walls, decking	rotary cut veneer	blind veneer
	musical instruments		modeling
	cabinetmaking		
	staircases		

ILOMBA *(Pycnanthus angolensis)*

Family:	*Myristicaceae*

Other Names:	*qualele, lolako, lomba*
Sierra Leone:	*dihin*
Liberia:	*gboyei*
Ivory Coast:	*walele*
Ghana:	*otie, esti*
Nigeria:	*akomu, ekom*
Cameroon:	*bosamba, bokondu*
Congo countries:	*bosengo, n'lolako, lifondo*
Angola:	*mutuje*

HABITAT

Ilomba's growth region extends throughout much of the continent's Atlantic region and into Central Africa. It is mainly found in humid evergreen rain forests, but occasionally also in transitional zones or drier, sparsely-wooded sections of the rain forest.

TREE DESCRIPTION

This quick-growing tree thrives on sunlight. It can be up to 40 m (131 ft) tall; its trunk diameter typically measures between 50–75 cm (1.5–2.5 ft) but infrequently can be as large as 100 cm (3.5 ft). The trunk is straight and cylindrical with about half its length clear of branches; small root buttresses are sometimes present.

WOOD DESCRIPTION

Ilomba sapwood and core wood are practically indistinguishable. The wood is initially a homogeneous pale pink to gray-brown, which may later darken to a strong dirt-brown color. A grayish-brown coloration my indicate the beginning stages of a fungus attack.

Durability Class	III	**E – Module**	8,200 N/mm²
Raw density	0.48 g/cm³	**Volume dwindle**	14.7 %
Bending strength	65 N/mm²	**Tangential shrinkage**	9.3 %
Compression strength	38 N/mm²	**Radial shrinkage**	4.8 %

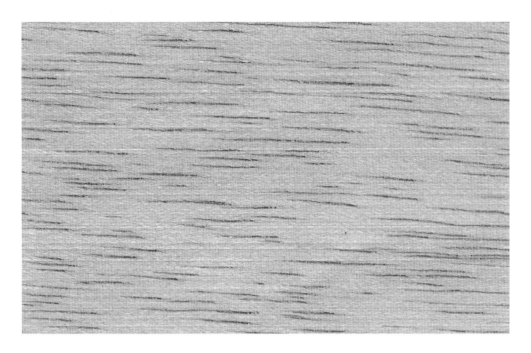

PROPERTIES AND APPLICATIONS

This moderately-light, soft, homogeneous wood has no outstanding physical properties other than its well-balanced strength characteristics. This structural balance makes ilomba an excellent choice for rotary cut and flat sawn veneer production, and it is used increasingly in Europe to manufacture plywood and battens. Note: it is very important to avoid importing the wood during the winter and summer seasons as frost causes fungus attacks and heat can cause cracking.

USES
Indoor

Very Good	Good	Usable	Not Usable
rotary cut veneer	plywood	intarsia works	construction wood
flat sawn veneer	blind veneer	cabinetmaking	furniture
	modeling		flooring
			walls, decking
			paneling
			musical instruments
			doors
			staircases
			window frames
			laboratory furniture & fittings
			ship, rail & truck building
			weapons industry

IROKO / KAMBALA *(Chlorophora excelsa)*

Family:	*Moraceae*
Other Names:	*kambala, African oak, chene d'afrique, odum*
Sierra Leone:	*katema*
Liberia:	*semli*
Nigeria:	*rokko*
Cameroon:	*abang*
Gabon:	*abang*
Congo countries:	*lusanga, mvule, molundu*
Angola:	*moreira*
Kenya:	*itule*

HABITAT
Iroko (also frequently called kambala) is one of tropical Africa's most common trees, with a territory extending like a belt across the middle of the continent. It is found in lower elevation evergreen rain forests, normally in clearings with an abundance of direct sunlight.

TREE DESCRIPTION
Iroko is an imposing giant of the primeval forest. Its trunk diameter is between 80–200 cm (2.5–6.5 ft), and its height ranges from 40–50 m (131–164 ft), up to 25 m (82 ft) of which may be clear of branches. It has inconsequential root buttresses.

WOOD DESCRIPTION
The sapwood is pale yellow—easily differentiated from the core wood whose color, in female trees, can vary from grayish-yellow to olive- or chocolate-brown. The wood of male trees is darker and can be similar in appearance to the olive-green wood of teak.

Durability Class	II	**E – Module**	9,900 N/mm^2
Raw density	0.65 – 0.70 g/cm^3	**Volume dwindle**	10.1 %
Bending strength	100 N/mm^2	**Tangential shrinkage**	5.6 %
Compression strength	57 N/mm^2	**Radial shrinkage**	3.5%

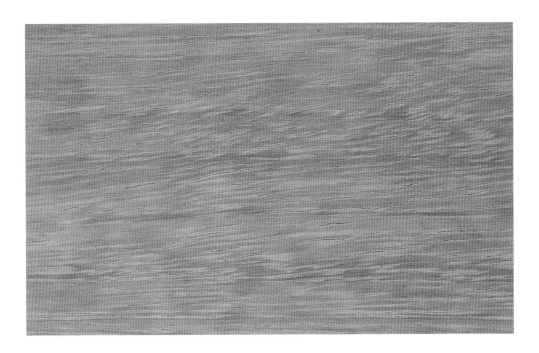

PROPERTIES AND APPLICATIONS

This is a hard and heavy timber with strength values very near to those of teak and oak. It is an outstanding general construction timber for both indoor and outdoor purposes and is also quite suitable for parquet, staircases, gateways, doors, and windows. Pieces with attractive striped markings are used for interior architectural panels. Iroko is also ideal for small carvings and intarsia works.

USES
Indoor/Outdoor

Very Good	Good	Usable	Not Usable
construction wood	furniture	laboratory furniture & fittings	musical instruments
flooring	paneling	rotary cut veneer	plywood
walls, decking	intarsia works	modeling	blind veneer
doors	cabinetmaking		
staircases	weapons industry		
window frames	flat sawn veneer		
ship, rail & truck building			

KEKELE *(Holoptelea grandis)*

Family:	*Ulmaceae*

Other Names:
Nigeria: *ulazo*
Cameroon: *awep*
Congo countries: *mbosso, gomboue, nemba-mbobolo*
Ivory Coast: *gore, gouedi*

HABITAT
Kekele is commonly found throughout West and Central Africa. It grows in semi-arid regions and dry areas of the savannah, preferring riverbank locations.

TREE DESCRIPTION
This deciduous tree can reach 30 m (98 ft) in height and achieve diameters of 80–110 cm (2.5–3.5 ft) or more. Its root buttresses tend to be short and sharp.

WOOD DESCRIPTION
The sapwood is little differentiated from the core wood, which is pale yellow-brown with a bit of luster. The wood has a homogeneous, medium-fine texture and may include alternating gleaming stripes. The growth rings are not easily distinguished from each other.

Durability Class	III	**E – Module**	12,000 N/mm²
Raw density	0.65 g/cm³	**Volume dwindle**	-
Bending strength	116 N/mm²	**Tangential shrinkage**	9.1 %
Compression strength	60 N/mm²	**Radial shrinkage**	4.6 %

PROPERTIES AND APPLICATIONS

Kekele is a fairly hard, solid tree with medium-heavy wood that can grow in either a straight or twisting fashion. The wood is somewhat tough, but quite flexible, tending to become coarser and slightly buckled over time; end and edge cracks are common. It is a versatile timber for interior projects and is also a good choice for woodturned goods, intarsia, veneers, and plywood.

USES

Indoor

Very Good	Good	Usable	Not Usable
	furniture	construction wood	musical instruments
	flooring	doors	plywood
	walls, decking	staircases	laboratory furniture & fittings
	paneling	window frames	ship, rail & truck building
	intarsia works		weapons industry
	cabinetmaking		blind veneer
	rotary cut veneer		modeling
	flat sawn veneer		

KELE *(Sapium ellipticum)*

Family:	*Euphorbiaceae*

Other Names:	*ebusok, alokwe*
D.R. of the Congo:	*kele*
Uganda:	*musasa*

HABITAT
Kele (also commonly known as alokwe) grows in the eastern region of the Democratic Republic of the Congo and, in small numbers, in Uganda. It is found in damp evergreen forests.

TREE DESCRIPTION
This rare tree species achieves a height of 25–30 m (82–98 ft) and a diameter of 60–90 cm (2–3 ft). The trunk is straight and cylindrical and has short root buttresses. A mature tree may contain some 15–20 m (49–66 ft) of usable timber.

WOOD DESCRIPTION
Kele sapwood is white with light-brown pores, and about 10 cm (3.9 in) thick; it has no useful applications. The core wood is light reddish-brown and resembles the bright makore (*Tieghemella heckelii; see separate reference*) that grows in the same area. Its grain is wavy and beautifully nuanced.

Durability Class	IV	**E – Module**	9,600 N/mm^2
Raw density	0.45 – 0.55 g/cm^3	**Volume dwindle**	6.8 %
Bending strength	65 N/mm^2	**Tangential shrinkage**	-
Compression strength	-	**Radial shrinkage**	-

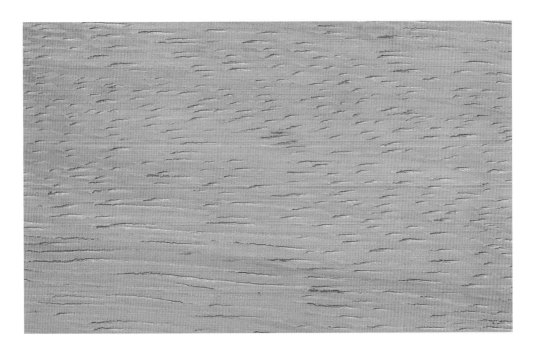

PROPERTIES AND APPLICATIONS

Kele is a light hardwood with moderate bending strength that, with repeated gluing, becomes very flexible. The wood splinters easily after drying, so surfaces should be properly treated to prevent this. Additionally, high humidity environments cause decomposition to occur, necessitating chemical treatment prior to shipping. Kele is used in the production of veneer and intarsia work, in the cabinetmaking industry, and in the construction of paneling. Further uses for the wood have not yet been sufficiently tested. In the furniture industry, kele may prove to be a good choice for solid front doors.

USES

Indoor

Very Good	Good	Usable	Not Usable
flat sawn veneer	walls, decking	furniture	construction wood
	paneling	flooring	staircases
	intarsia works	musical instruments	window frames
	cabinetmaking	plywood	laboratory furniture & fittings
	rotary cut veneer	doors	ship, rail & truck building
		blind veneer	weapons industry
		modeling	

KHAYA, ACAJOU D'AFRIQUE *(Khaya anthotheca)*

Family: *Meliaceae*

Other Names: *acajou d'Afrique,*
African mahogany
Ivory Coast: *krala, ira*
Ghana: *ahafo*
Cameroon: *mangona*
Uganda: *munyama*
Congo countries: *khaya-mahogany*

HABITAT

Khaya anthotheca is the first of four khaya (mahogany) varieties discussed in this book. It is often found just beyond the coastal regions of much of tropical Africa (starting some 80 km (50 miles) inland). The species' favored habitat is the dry eastern area of the West African savannah. It can be found grouped with other *Meliaceae* varieties or growing singly.

TREE DESCRIPTION

Khaya anthotheca is a small, slight tree not exceeding 30 m (98 ft) in height, with a maximum diameter of about 100 cm (3.5 ft). The trunk is cylindrical and branchless, with the base exhibiting tall, strongly developed root buttresses.

WOOD DESCRIPTION

The core wood is light salmon-red and clearly differentiated from the thin and more lightly colored sapwood. Its pores are medium-sized and few in number; they are either individually scattered or grouped in pairs. On a longitudinal cut, they appear as dark grooves, which are frequently filled with a black or red substance (resin, possibly mixed with calcium deposits).

Durability Class	III	E – Module	8,300 N/mm^2
Raw density	0.56 g/cm^3	**Volume dwindle**	11.8 %
Bending strength	88 N/mm^2	**Tangential shrinkage**	6.0 %
Compression strength	50 N/mm^2	**Radial shrinkage**	4.3 %

PROPERTIES AND APPLICATIONS

Khaya anthotheca is a member of the highly functional African mahogany family. It is very well-suited for both furniture manufacturing and veneering. Particularly popular are veneers made from wood cut from the trunk fork (known as khaya crotch); these rare and expensive veneers are highly valued by the furniture industry. Artists and carpenters use *Khaya anthotheca* for creating various works of art such as cigar boxes, microscope cases, model aircraft, and any manner of decorative work. It is considered a good alternative to the meranti timber of Southeast Asia and thus is suitable for window frame manufacturing.

USES

Indoor

Very Good	Good	Usable	Not Usable
furniture	paneling	construction wood	ship, rail & truck building
cabinetmaking	intarsia works	flooring	
rotary cut veneer	doors	walls, decking	
flat sawn veneer	staircases	musical instruments	
	window frames	plywood	
		laboratory furniture & fittings	
		weapons industry	
		blind veneer	
		modeling	

KHAYA CAILCEDRAT
(Khaya senegalensis, Khaya grandifolia)

Family:	*Meliaceae*
Other Names:	*African mahogany, acajou cailcedrat, bissilon*
Ivory Coast:	*acajou a grandes feuilles*
Ghana:	*kuka*
Nigeria:	*undianunu, kalungi, oganwo, bandora, bele, bogu*
Guinea Bissau:	*bissilon*
Benin:	*kalungi*

HABITAT
Khaya cailcedrat is found in West Africa from Senegal to Cameroon. It mainly grows in groups in the dry regions of the western savannah but can occasionally be found growing individually in the Sudan and Ethiopia.

TREE DESCRIPTION
This variety of khaya is small in stature with a height of no more than 25 m (82 ft) and a diameter of 60–90 cm (2–3 ft). Root buttresses are either minimal or non-existent. The trunk grows irregularly and provides at most some 6 m (20 ft) of usable timber.

WOOD DESCRIPTION
It has a dark red or reddish-brown color, which contrasts with the thin, more bright-ly-colored sapwood. The core wood can darken to a purple- or reddish-brown color. The fiber is very irregular, thereby slightly decreasing the wood's firmness.

Durability Class	II	E – Module	10,000 N/mm²
Raw density	0.60 – 0.75 g/cm³	**Volume dwindle**	12.4 %
Bending strength	96 N/mm²	**Tangential shrinkage**	6.5 %
Compression strength	53 N/mm²	**Radial shrinkage**	5.8 %

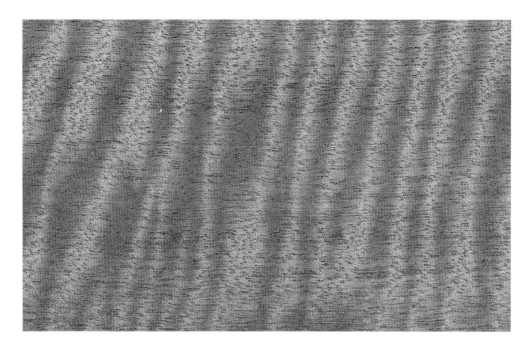

PROPERTIES AND APPLICATIONS

Khaya cailcedrat is the hardest and heaviest of the African mahoganies. Both *Khaya senegalensis* and *Khaya grandifolia* have good physical properties and are resistant to weather, insects and decomposition. The veneer industry prefers *Khaya senegalensis* because of its beautiful grain, but both types are popular choices for cabinetmaking and the production of luxury furniture, flooring, stairs, doors and windows.

USES

Indoor/Outdoor

Very Good	Good	Usable	Not Usable
cabinetmaking	construction wood	walls, decking	musical instruments
flat sawn veneer	furniture	paneling	plywood
	flooring	intarsia works	weapons industry
	doors	laboratory furniture & fittings	blind veneer
	staircases	rotary cut veneer	
	window frames	modeling	
	ship, rail & truck building		

KHAYA MAHOGANY *(Khaya ivorensis)*

Family:	*Meliaceae*
Other Names:	*African mahogany, acajou de bassam*
Ivory Coast:	*dubb, doukoma, dugura*
Ghana:	*sekundimahogany*
Cameroon:	*acajou rouge, n'gollon*
Nigeria:	*ogwango, lagosmahogany*
Congo countries:	*n'dola*
Gabon:	*m'bega, ombega*

HABITAT
Khaya ivorensis is the most commonly exported type of African mahogany. It can be found in the damp rain forests of West Africa, with a territory extending from Senegal in the west to the Congo region in the east. It usually grows with other *Meliaceae* varieties (*Khaya* or otherwise), often in small scattered groups.

TREE DESCRIPTION
Khaya mahogany can achieve heights of more than 45 m (148 ft) and diameters between 100–200 cm (3.5–6.5 ft). The trunk is cylindrical and free of branches, the lower segment being buttressed by high, thick roots.

WOOD DESCRIPTION
The sapwood of *Khaya ivorensis* is thin and light-colored, while the clearly differentiated core wood can be any number of shades of red. The pores are medium-sized and either scattered individually or grouped in pairs. On a longitudinal cut they appear as dark grooves, which are frequently filled with a black or red substance (resin, possibly mixed with calcium deposits).

Durability Class	II	E – Module	9,800 N/mm^2
Raw density	0.51 g/cm^3	Volume dwindle	9.1 %
Bending strength	85 N/mm^2	Tangential shrinkage	5.7 %
Compression strength	45 N/mm^2	Radial shrinkage	3.2 %

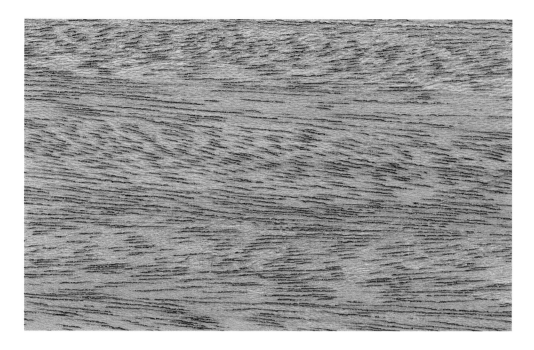

PROPERTIES AND APPLICATIONS

Khaya ivorensis, like other members of the popular and versatile African mahogany family, is an excellent choice for furniture production and veneering. Particularly popular are veneers (often marketed as drape, moiré and pommele veneers) from the trunk fork, or khaya-crotch; these are highly valued by the furniture industry, and their rarity makes them very expensive. The wood has good resistance to the weather and to insect attacks.

USES
Indoor/Outdoor

Very Good	Good	Usable	Not Usable
furniture	flooring	construction wood	
cabinetmaking	walls, decking	plywood	
rotary cut veneer	paneling	laboratory furniture & fittings	
flat sawn veneer	intarsia works	ship, rail & truck building	
	musical instruments	weapons industry	
	doors	blind veneer	
	staircases	modeling	
	window frames		

KHAYA / UMBAUA *(Khaya nyasica)*

Family:	*Meliaceae*

Other Names:	*nyasaland mahogany*
Cameroon:	*ilulu*
Cabinda:	*muhaua*
Kenya:	*m'baua*
Tanzania:	*mwawa, mkangazi*
D.R. of the Congo:	*mutonde, mbamba*
Belgium:	*mululu*

HABITAT

Khaya umbaua is widely distributed throughout East Africa with major concentrations of the tree located in the southeastern region of the continent. This mahogany variety grows in dry, bare forest tracts and isolated areas of the rain forest.

TREE DESCRIPTION

Khaya nyasica is the smallest of the khaya trees with a height of 25–30 m (82–98 ft). However, the diameter can reach a robust 150 cm (5 ft), although measurements of 60–120 cm (2–4 ft) are more common. The trunk is straight, cylindrical, and clear of branches to approximately 18 m (59 ft).

WOOD DESCRIPTION

The white-pink sapwood is strongly differentiated from the dark pinkish-red core wood; after exposure to air, the wood darkens to a gold-red-brown coloration. It is anatomically very similar to its sister variety *Khaya anthotheca*. Khaya umbaua has very long fibers and is the heaviest wood of the khaya family.

Durability Class	II	E – Module	10,000 N/mm²
Raw density	0.65 – 0.75 g/cm³	Volume dwindle	9.0 %
Bending strength	85 N/mm²	Tangential shrinkage	5.5 %
Compression strength	45 N/mm²	Radial shrinkage	3.0 %

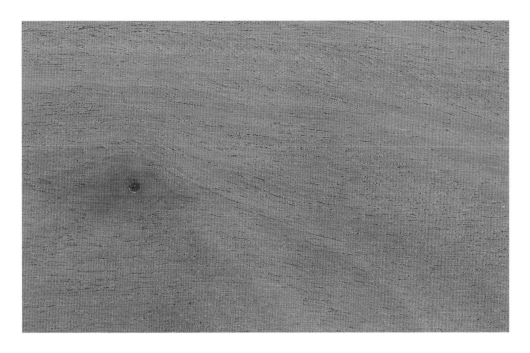

PROPERTIES AND APPLICATIONS

Khaya nyasica is a durable, medium-hard wood that suffers only slight shrinkage, and is weather- and insect-resistant. Its physical properties are approximately 20 percent superior to *Khaya anthotheca*. It can be processed by every veneer technology and as solid wood, is used to produce furniture, doors and window frames. It is also used as construction timber for projects such as building railway cars.

USES

Indoor/Outdoor

Very Good	Good	Usable	Not Usable
furniture	construction wood	intarsia works	flooring
rotary cut veneer	walls, decking	musical instruments	plywood
flat sawn veneer	paneling	staircases	
	cabinetmaking	laboratory furniture & fittings	
	doors	weapons industry	
	window frames	blind veneer	
	ship, rail & truck building	modeling	

KOSIPO *(Entandrophragma candollei)*

Family:	*Meliaceae*
Other Names:	*heavy sapele*
D.R. of the Congo:	*impopo, lifaki*
Rep. of the Congo:	*mpembe*
Angola:	*lifuko*
Ivory Coast:	*boubousson*
Ghana:	*akowaa*
Cameroon:	*klatie*

HABITAT
Kosipo is a rare species located in sections of Central Africa. It is a slow growing, shade-favoring tree found in both the rain forest and the savannah. Specimens from the eastern region of the Democratic Republic of the Congo tend to be of somewhat higher quality.

TREE DESCRIPTION
This large tree can reach heights of approximately 40–50 m (131–164 ft). The straight, cylindrical trunk can be 200 cm (6.5 ft) thick, with a usable timber length of up to 25 m (82 ft). There are extensive root buttresses.

WOOD DESCRIPTION
The sapwood is grayish-yellow, about 5 cm (2 in) thick, and contrasts sharply in color with the dark reddish-brown core wood (which frequently darkens upon air exposure to become violet-brown). Kosipo is a straight-fibered, medium-density wood, with a rough, porous texture. The pores are often filled with resin.

Durability Class	I	E – Module	11,800 N/mm^2
Raw density	0.69 g/cm^3	Volume dwindle	12.0 %
Bending strength	102 N/mm^2	Tangential shrinkage	6.0 %
Compression strength	57 N/mm^2	Radial shrinkage	4.3 %

PROPERTIES AND APPLICATIONS

Kosipo is suitable for staircases, banisters, flooring, and flat sawn veneers for doors and furniture. It is also used for decorative paneling and artistic wood-working. Transparent or clear varnish is recommended for surface treatment; optimal wood humidity is 12-14 percent.

USES

Indoor

Very Good	Good	Usable	Not Usable
flooring	furniture	construction wood	plywood
paneling	walls, decking	musical instruments	ship, rail & truck building
intarsia works	doors	window frames	blind veneer
cabinetmaking	staircases	laboratory furniture & fittings	
	flat sawn veneer	weapons industry	
		rotary cut veneer	
		modeling	

KOTO *(Pterygota macrocarpa)*

Family:	*Sterculiaceae*

Other Names:	*pterygota*
Cameroon:	*efok, kion*
Ivory Coast:	*bofo ouale, bontue, pohouro*
Gabon:	*ake*
D.R. of the Congo:	*ikame*
Ghana:	*awari, kyre*
Nigeria:	*poroporo, kefe*
Germany:	*antolia*

HABITAT
Koto is found growing in damp West African forests from Ivory Coast to the Congo basin (the species also exists in Asia). *Pterygota* is botanically related to the cola nut tree (*Cola nitida*).

TREE DESCRIPTION
This medium-sized tree has a height of 25–40 m (82–131 ft) and a diameter of 60–110 cm (2–3.5 ft). There is typically a trunk section of some 20 m (66 ft) that is cylindrical and free of branches. Root buttresses are often low to the ground, but in wetter areas may be many feet high.

WOOD DESCRIPTION
The sapwood and core wood are barely differentiated. The core wood is yellowish or ivory-hued, darkening after being cut to a reddish-brown or gray-yellow-brown color. Freshly cut koto has an unpleasant smell. The wood consists of very small fibers and bears a structural resemblance to eyong (*Sterculia tragacantha; see separate reference*).

Durability Class	IV	**E – Module**	9,000 N/mm^2
Raw density	0.53 g/cm^3	**Volume dwindle**	11.9 %
Bending strength	84 N/mm^2	**Tangential shrinkage**	7.7 %
Compression strength	50 N/mm^2	**Radial shrinkage**	4.0 %

PROPERTIES AND APPLICATIONS

Koto must be dried in a slow and careful manner to avoid tearing or breakage, and should be chemically treated prior to transportation. It is susceptible to insect attack, mold, fungus, and the effects of weather. The wood is quite workable and responsive to gluing; however, its poor durability makes it unsuitable for exterior purposes. Common uses include a variety of interior applications, plywood production, and the manufacture of blind and decorative veneers.

USES

Indoor

Very Good	Good	Usable	Not Usable
plywood	rotary cut veneer	furniture	construction wood
flat sawn veneer	modeling	walls, decking	flooring
blind veneer		paneling	intarsia works
		musical instruments	staircases
		cabinetmaking	window frames
		doors	laboratory furniture & fittings
			ship, rail & truck building
			weapons industry

KUMBI *(Lannea welwitschii)*

Family:	*Anacardiaceae*

Other Names:	*onzabili*
D.R. of the Congo:	*kumbi*

HABITAT
Kumbi—also known as onzabili—is found in tropical Africa, its habitat stretching from Ivory Coast to the Democratic Republic of the Congo.

TREE DESCRIPTION
The lower trunk is slim, cylindrical, and well-formed. In regions where favorable conditions exist, the bole can be free of branches for up to 30 m (98 ft). Trunk diameters normally range from 50–80 cm (1.5–2.5 ft) but are known to reach as much as 150 cm (5 ft).

WOOD DESCRIPTION
The core wood and sapwood are little differentiated—both have a grayish-pink to light-red color, frequently with a pearly sheen on cut surfaces. The texture is somewhat rough, although often with patches that have a felt-like feel to them. There can be substantial variations in the grain, as the tree is prone to twisting growth patterns.

Durability Class	III	**E – Module**	10,500 N/mm²
Raw density	0.66 g/cm³	**Volume dwindle**	13.3 %
Bending strength	115 N/mm²	**Tangential shrinkage**	6.8 %
Compression strength	53 N/mm²	**Radial shrinkage**	4.3 %

PROPERTIES AND APPLICATIONS

This soft but heavy wood has good strength properties. Kumbi is, however, neither weather- nor insect-resistant, and it is very important that the wood be chemically treated prior to shipping. It suffers moderate shrinkage. Kumbi's flexibility makes it a good choice for rotary-cut veneers. There is some demand for the wood as construction material for interior works; it is also used for carving, moldings, and frames.

USES

Indoor

Very Good	Good	Usable	Not Usable
	flooring	furniture	construction wood
	walls, decking	paneling	musical instruments
	intarsia works	plywood	cabinetmaking
	rotary cut veneer	door	staircases
	flat sawn veneer	blind veneer	window frames
		modeling	laboratory furniture & fittings
			ship, rail & truck building
			weapons industry

LATI *(Amphimas pterocarpoides)*

Family: *Caesalpinaceae*

Other Names: *white wenge*
D.R. of the Congo: *bokanga*
Rep. of the Congo: *muizi*
Cameroon: *edjin, edzil*
Gabon: *edzui*

HABITAT
Lati exists in both humid evergreen forests and drier wooded tracts ranging from Cameroon to the central region of the Democratic Republic of the Congo.

TREE DESCRIPTION
The tree can grow to 50 m (164 ft) tall with a diameter of 120 cm (4 ft). The trunk is straight and cylindrical with root buttresses at the base. An identifying characteristic of lati is that its trunk is covered by a thin, smooth bark which exudes a red sap.

WOOD DESCRIPTION
The thick sapwood has a light pinkish-brown color which contrasts clearly with the darker yellowish-brown core wood. The grain is mostly straight with some irregularities. The occasional structural twists are often accompanied with a corresponding stripe in the wood.

Durability Class	III	E – Module	13,000 N/mm²
Raw density	0.80 g/cm³	Volume dwindle	18.0 %
Bending strength	126 N/mm²	Tangential shrinkage	12.1 %
Compression strength	52 N/mm²	Radial shrinkage	6.8 %

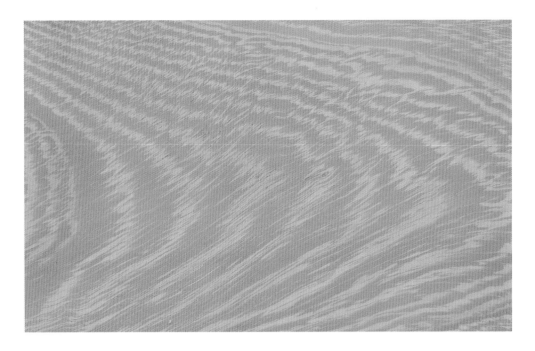

PROPERTIES AND APPLICATIONS

Lati is a hard, solid timber that is largely unworkable with hand tools. This versatile wood's uses include flooring and general construction. It is also used to produce veneers (although extensive steaming is a necessary preparatory step); with slight color modifications, the wood can be used as a substitute for oak furniture paneling. As lati is relatively new on the market, its properties and best uses have not been fully proven.

USES

Indoor

Very Good	Good	Usable	Not Usable
	flooring	furniture	construction wood
	walls, decking	paneling	musical instruments
	intarsia works	plywood	cabinetmaking
	rotary cut veneer	door	staircases
	flat sawn veneer	blind veneer	window frames
		modeling	laboratory furniture & fittings
			ship, rail & truck building
			weapons industry

LIMBA *(Terminalia superba)*

Family:	*Combretaceae*

Other Names:	*frake, limba noir*
Cameroon:	*akom*
Equatorial-Guinea:	*akom*
Ghana:	*framo, elblale*
Congo countries:	*limbo, ndima*
Sierra Leone:	*bagi*
Liberia:	*baye*
Ivory Coast:	*fram-tra*

HABITAT
Limba is Africa's most commonly found and widely-used timber. This fast-growing tree typically dwells in rain forests and savannah regions, frequently growing in groups. It is distributed throughout much of tropical West Africa, from Sierra Leone to the Congo basin.

TREE DESCRIPTION
Limba is a large tree, up to 45 m (148 ft) tall with a diameter between 50–110 cm (1.5–3.5 ft). The trunk is straight and cylindrical, usually with root buttresses up to 3 m (10 ft) in height. It is clear of branches up to 30 m (98 ft).

WOOD DESCRIPTION
The sapwood and core wood are usually both dark yellow; however, in some older trunks the core wood becomes grayish- or blackish-brown and may possess an olive-colored luster. Upon drying, the wood takes on a much darker appearance, resembling North American walnut, and is often marketed as limba noir.

Durability Class	III	**E – Module**	11,000 N/mm²
Raw density	0.55 g/cm³	**Volume dwindle**	15.3 – 21.0 %
Bending strength	95 N/mm²	**Tangential shrinkage**	10.0 %
Compression strength	48 N/mm²	**Radial shrinkage**	5.3 %

PROPERTIES AND APPLICATIONS

Limba has physical properties similar to European oak: although the wood is fragile, it is also very flexible and possesses good impact and pressure strengths. Drying is a trouble-free process, but limba is quite susceptible to insects. Its uses include the production of plywood, cabinets, and veneers. Repeated gluing is necessary when it is used for projects such as the construction of doors and flooring.

USES
Indoor

Very Good	Good	Usable	Not Usable
plywood	paneling	construction wood	intarsia works
blind veneer	cabinetmaking	furniture	musical instruments
	rotary cut veneer	flooring	staircases
	flat sawn veneer	walls, decking	window frames
	modeling	doors	laboratory furniture & fittings
			ship, rail & truck building
			weapons industry

LIMBALI *(Gilbertiodendron dewevrei)*

Family:	*Caesalpinaceae*

Other Names: *ditchipi*
Nigeria: *ekogoi, otabu*
Cameroon: *ekobem*
Congo countries: *balu, bolapa, kombulu, wete, ligudu*

HABITAT
Limbali is found most frequently in Central Africa, particularly in the countries of Cameroon, the Republic of the Congo, and the Democratic Republic of the Congo. It flourishes in sandy soil such as that sometimes found on mountainsides or at river shores. The tree thrives on seasonal rains, but is rarely found in routinely flooded zones.

TREE DESCRIPTION
Limbali has an average height of 25 m (82 ft) with a diameter of 60–100 cm (2–3.5 ft). The trunk is straight, well-formed, and branchless for up to half its length. Those specimens over 30 m (98 ft) tall have about 25 m (82 ft) of usable timber.

WOOD DESCRIPTION
Limbali is a beautiful wood, reddish-brown in color and partially veined with dark streaks. The sapwood is up to 10 cm thick (4 in) with colors varying from light yellow or gray to pale brown; it is clearly differentiated from the core wood. In the longitudinal cut, chains of straight, regularly-arranged pores will be displayed.

Durability Class	I	E – Module	12,000 N/mm²
Raw density	0.81 g/cm³	**Volume dwindle**	16.1 %
Bending strength	150 N/mm²	**Tangential shrinkage**	9.8 %
Compression strength	72 N/mm²	**Radial shrinkage**	4.8 %

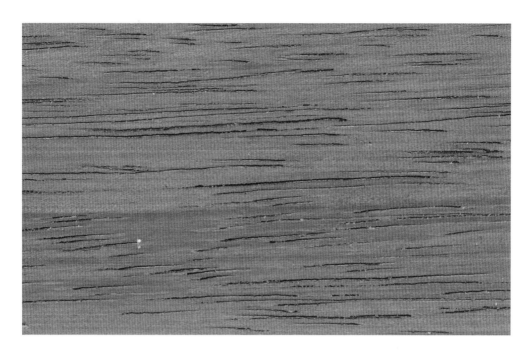

PROPERTIES AND APPLICATIONS

Limbali, due to it dense structure, has very good technical properties and high strength values. It is durable and weather- and insect-resistant. However, the wood does have a tendency to crack during the drying process. Its qualities make it an outstanding choice for the production of window frames, doorframes, staircases, flooring, and decking.

USES

Indoor/Outdoor

Very Good	Good	Usable	Not Usable
flooring	construction wood	laboratory furniture & fittings	musical instruments
walls, decking	furniture	ship, rail & truck building	plywood
doors	paneling	weapons industry	blind veneer
staircases	intarsia works	rotary cut veneer	
	cabinetmaking	modeling	
	window frames		
	flat sawn veneer		

LONGHI / ANIGRE
(Gambeya lacourtiana, Gambeya albida, Gambeya gigantea)

Family:	*Sapotaceae*
Other Names:	*grogoli, koandio, osam*
Congo countries:	*longui, bohambi*
Cameroon:	*abam*
Gabun:	*M'bebame*

HABITAT
Longhi is found in humid formations throughout West and Central Africa, from Ivory Coast to the Congo basin. Other *Gambeya* species are found in all tropical and subtropical regions of the earth.

TREE DESCRIPTION
Longhi trees are between 30–40 m (98–131 ft) in height (with a wide lush crown) and are branchless for up to 16 m (52 ft). Trunk diameters range from 60–130 cm (2–4.5 ft); the bole is straight and cylindrical with well-developed root buttresses.

WOOD DESCRIPTION
There are no distinctive differences between the sapwood and core wood. The appearance is normally reddish, although oxidation can create a darker reddish-brown coloration.

Durability Class	III	E – Module	11,000 N/mm²
Raw density	0.55 – 0.75 g/cm³	Volume dwindle	11.3 %
Bending strength	100 N/mm²	Tangential shrinkage	7.4 %
Compression strength	60 N/mm²	Radial shrinkage	3.8 %

PROPERTIES AND APPLICATIONS

This is a moderately hard, dense timber with good mechanical strength proper-ties. Drying should be done quickly to prevent the wood from taking on an undesirable dark or grayish appearance. It is a satisfactory general construction wood that can also be used for a variety of artistic carpentry purposes such as cre-ating solid-wood furniture. Longhi's natural coloring makes it a popular choice for flat sawn veneers. In preparation for flat sawn veneer production, the wood should be carefully steamed at approximately 85° C (185° F) to prevent cracking.

USES

Indoor

Very Good	Good	Usable	Not Usable
furniture	construction wood	staircases	musical instruments
cabinetmaking	flooring	window frames	plywood
doors	walls, decking		laboratory furniture & fittings
flat sawn veneer	paneling		ship, rail & truck building
	intarsia works		rotary cut veneer
	weapons industry		blind veneer
			modeling

LOTOFA *(Sterculia rhinopetala)*

Family: *Sterculiaceae*

Other Names: *red sterculia*
Cameroon: *n'kanang, bojanga*
Ghana: *wawabima, awasea*
Nigeria: *aye, orodo, otutu, ekko*

HABITAT
Lotofa can be found along the entire West African coast, growing in damp ever-green forests as well as the drier forests of the savannah.

TREE DESCRIPTION
This species grows to 30 m (98 ft) in height and has diameters of 60–80 cm (2–2.5 ft). The trunk is cylindrical, clear of branches for up to 20 m (66 ft), and has narrow root buttresses. Reddish-brown hairy branches are a characteristic of this wood.

WOOD DESCRIPTION
The yellow-gray sapwood is approximately 7 cm (3 in) thick and clearly demar-cated from the core wood, which is red or dark red with brownish-black stripes. The fibers are long and fine, and the wood has a beautiful gloss.

Durability Class	III	**E – Module**	15,000 N/mm²
Raw density	0.70 – 0.80 g/cm³	**Volume dwindle**	15.0 – 21.0 %
Bending strength	150 N/mm²	**Tangential shrinkage**	10.0 %
Compression strength	72 N/mm²	**Radial shrinkage**	5.5 %

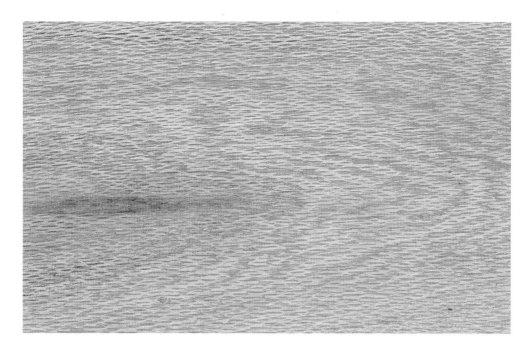

PROPERTIES AND APPLICATIONS

This hard and heavy wood has moderate flexibility and physical properties; it is not very durable. After sawing the wood, a chemical treatment should be applied to prevent insect attack and fungus growth. Because of lotofa's pronounced tendency to shrink, drying must be executed in a slow and careful manner to prevent splitting and cracking. Strong, high-quality tools are required to work this wood. Lotofa is used for such things as interior fittings, furniture, panels and floors.

USES
Indoor

Very Good	Good	Usable	Not Usable
	furniture	construction wood	musical instruments
	flooring	intarsia works	plywood
	walls, decking	cabinetmaking	window frames
	paneling	doors	laboratory furniture & fittings
		staircases	blind veneer
		ship, rail & truck building	modeling
		weapons industry	
		rotary cut veneer	
		flat sawn veneer	

MADAGASCAR-PALISSANDRE
(Dalbergia baroni) or *(Dalbergia pterocarpifolia)*

Family: *Fabaceae*

Other Names: *voamboana*
Madagascar: *palissandre de tamatave*

HABITAT
These two closely related tree species are found in the eastern region of Madagascar, primarily in the north. They thrive in damp evergreen forests.

TREE DESCRIPTION
The trees can achieve heights of up to 50 m (164 ft). *Dalbergia baroni* has the larger diameter of the two—up to 80 cm (2.5 ft)—whereas *Dalbergia pterocarpifolia* has a maximum diameter of about 40 cm (1.5 ft). Neither type evidences root buttresses.

WOOD DESCRIPTION
In both species the sapwood is very thin with a maximum thickness of 4 cm (1.5 in). The color of *Dalbergia baroni's* core wood is violet to black-violet; *Dalbergia pterocarpifolia's* color is more reddish. The grain has a wavy structure that lends a beautiful, rather ornamental look to the wood.

Durability Class	II	E – Module	16,200 N/mm²
Raw density	0.75 – 0.95 g/cm³	Volume dwindle	8.8 – 13.0 %
Bending strength	152 – 185 N/mm²	Tangential shrinkage	5.5 – 7.5 %
Compression strength	71 – 101 N/mm²	Radial shrinkage	3.0 – 4.0 %

PROPERTIES AND APPLICATIONS

Madagscar-pallisandre possesses the same good technical and physical properties as its sister species in Asia and South America and has been compared with oak. It is naturally durable, and the core wood is weather- and insect-resistant. The drying process is typically performed without difficulty. This wood is used to produce furniture, panels, flat sawn veneers, and intarsia works. Local inhabitants often create works of art with it.

USES
Indoor/Outdoor

Very Good	Good	Usable	Not Usable
furniture	walls, decking	construction wood	plywood
flooring	paneling	doors	laboratory furniture & fittings
intarsia works	musical instruments	staircases	ship, rail & truck building
cabinetmaking		window frames	blind veneer
flat sawn veneer		weapons industry	modeling
		rotary cut veneer	

MAKORÉ *(Tieghemella heckelii)*

Family: *Sapotaceae*

Other Names: *oben mahogany*
Ghana: *abam, maori*
Nigeria: *aganokwe*
D.R. of the Congo: *kondofindo*

HABITAT
Makoré is a rare species growing mainly in east Liberia. In a 900 acre tract, one will find no more than twenty trees with a diameter of 90 cm (2 ft) or more. The occasional specimen will be encountered in other tropical West African nations, and significant numbers have recently been discovered in the eastern region of the Democratic Republic of the Congo. The tree's environment of preference is the humid evergreen forest.

TREE DESCRIPTION
Makoré reaches heights of 50 m (164 ft) or more; the trunk diameter varies between 80–220 m (2.5–7 ft). The bole is almost cylindrical and can be branchless for up to 30 m (98 ft). Roots buttresses, if present, are insignificant.

WOOD DESCRIPTION
The sapwood and core wood are clearly differentiated. The former, which can be up to 12 cm (4.5 in) thick, is a light grayish-pink or pale yellow color, while the heartwood varies from light reddish-brown to dark-brown. Its propensity for twisting, irregular growth patterns makes the wood a desirable source for decorative veneers and intarsia.

Durability Class	III	E – Module	12,000 N/mm²
Raw density	0.69 g/cm³	Volume dwindle	13.4 %
Bending strength	99 N/mm²	Tangential shrinkage	7.8 %
Compression strength	53 N/mm²	Radial shrinkage	5.9 %

PROPERTIES AND APPLICATIONS

Makoré is a solid, moderately heavy wood with good dynamic strength properties. It is very popular in the veneer industry, in part due to its small shrinkage rate. Makoré also has a number of solid-wood applications, including chair and shelf construction, staircases and railings, windows, and boat manufacturing.

USES

Indoor/Outdoor

Very Good	Good	Usable	Not Usable
	furniture	construction wood	plywood
	flooring	intarsia works	laboratory furniture & fittings
	walls, decking	weapons industry	ship, rail & truck building
	paneling	blind veneer	
	musical instruments	modeling	
	cabinetmaking		
	doors		
	staircases		
	window frames		
	rotary cut veneer		
	flat sawn veneer		

MECRUSSE *(Androstachys johnsonii)*

Family:	*Euphorbiaceae*
Other Names:	*lekombo ironwood*
Mozambique:	*mezimbite, cimbirre*
Swaziland:	*umbu kungu*
South Africa:	*uziibite, umbitzan*

HABITAT
Mecrusse grows in the rain forests of Southeast Africa, particularly in the mountainous regions of Mozambique. It is found in smaller quantities in Zimbabwe, South Africa and Swaziland.

TREE DESCRIPTION
The tree attains heights between 20–30 m (66–98 ft). The trunk grows very straight and cylindrically, with about 10–15 m (33–49 ft) of usable timber; diameters vary between 40–90 cm (1.5–3 ft).

WOOD DESCRIPTION
Mecrusse sapwood is narrow—only 15 mm (.5 in) thick—and has a whitish-yellow color. The core wood's coloration is light to dark reddish-brown; its grain is characteristically wavy.

Durability Class	I	E – Module	17,500 N/mm^2
Raw density	0.92 g/cm^3	Volume dwindle	11.8 %
Bending strength	145 N/mm^2	Tangential shrinkage	6.6 %
Compression strength	67 N/mm^2	Radial shrinkage	6.1 %

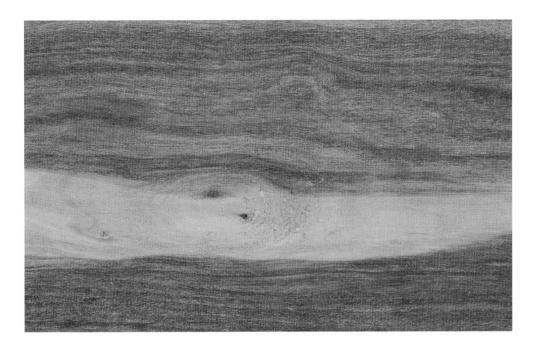

PROPERTIES AND APPLICATIONS

Mecrusse is a hard, strong and exceptionally durable wood. Drying must be performed slowly to prevent cracking and tearing, and kiln drying must not be done at overly high temperatures. The timber's toughness and resistance to weather and insects make it a common choice for applications such as flooring, railway sleepers and, in the past, telegraph poles. It is now typically used for heavy construction projects such as bridges and support beams for mines.

USES
Indoor/Outdoor

Very Good	Good	Usable	Not Usable
construction wood	ship, rail & truck building	walls, decking	furniture
flooring		doors	paneling
		flat sawn veneer	intarsia works
			musical instruments
			cabinetmaking
			plywood
			staircases
			window frames
			laboratory furniture & fittings
			weapons industry
			rotary cut veneer
			blind veneer
			modeling

MOABI *(Baillonella toxisperma)*

Family:	*Sapotaceae*
Other Names:	*njabi, African pearwood*
Cameroon:	*Cameroon makoré, adjab*
Gabon:	*adza, orere*

HABITAT
Moabi grows singly or in small groups in evergreen rain forests. Its habitat stretches from Nigeria to Cabinda; the largest quantities are found in Cameroon, where the species is commonly referred to as the Cameroon makoré or the so-called African pear tree.

TREE DESCRIPTION
Moabi, like makoré (*Thieghemella heckelli*) and douka (*Thieghemella africana*), is among the larger trees in West Africa. It achieves heights of up to 50 m (164 ft) with diameters of 80–240 cm (2.5–8 ft). The bark alone is approximately 5 cm (2 in) thick. A single tree can yield up to 20 cubic meters (8,480 board feet) of usable wood.

WOOD DESCRIPTION
The pinkish-white or gray colored sapwood is up to 7 cm (3 in) thick. The core wood is dark reddish-brown, often with violet coloring, and the grain is fine and straight.

Durability Class	II	E – Module	15,000 N/mm²
Raw density	0.88 g/cm³	Volume dwindle	12.8 %
Bending strength	150 N/mm²	Tangential shrinkage	8.0 %
Compression strength	68 N/mm²	Radial shrinkage	5.8 %

PROPERTIES AND APPLICATIONS

This heavy, medium-hard wood possesses good physical properties and is durable, weatherproof, and insect-resistant. Air-drying can be a lengthy process; kiln drying is faster but must be carefully executed to avoid cracking. Moabi can be used as both interior and exterior construction timber, often even without wood preservatives. It is also used to create luxury flooring and, being flexible and bendable, is popular with furniture manufacturers (particularly in chair production). Additionally, moabi is in high demand in the veneer industry. The wood is easily workable for this purpose but must be properly steamed beforehand. Incorrect steaming may result in discoloration.

USES
Indoor/Outdoor

Very Good	Good	Usable	Not Usable
construction wood	furniture	walls, decking	musical instruments
flooring	doors	paneling	plywood
ship, rail & truck building	staircases	intarsia works	blind veneer
	rotary cut veneer	cabinetmaking	
	flat sawn veneer	window frames	
		laboratory furniture & fittings	
		weapons industry	
		modeling	

MOVINGUI *(Distemonanthus benthamianus)*

Family:	*Ceasalpiniaceae*
Other Names:	*ayan*
Nigeria:	*Nigerian satinwood, anyaran*
Ghana:	*duabei, bonsamdua*
Cameroon:	*eyen*

HABITAT

Movingui mostly grows in the damp evergreen forests along the Gulf of Guinea into the Congo region; it is also occasionally found in drier areas. The tree normally grows apart from other of its species. Commercial interest in movingui is increasing, mainly because of its attractive color.

TREE DESCRIPTION

Movingui grows to heights of up to 40 m (131 ft), with diameters ranging from 60–80 cm (2–2.5 ft). The trunk is cylindrical, straight, and clear of branches for up to 20 m (66 ft). The tree has small root buttresses.

WOOD DESCRIPTION

The sapwood is only some 3 cm (1 in) wide and has a dirty yellowish-gray appearance. The core wood is a beautiful lemon-yellow or golden color; later, after being cut, it takes on a resplendent greenish color resembling that of the American satinwood (*Fagara flava*). Modest dark stripes may also be present. Crystalline deposits will sometimes be found in pores, and in the radial cut yellow-green streaks may be visible.

Durability Class	II	E – Module	11,300 N/mm^2
Raw density	0.71 g/cm^3	Volume dwindle	11.5 %
Bending strength	115 N/mm^2	Tangential shrinkage	6.2 %
Compression strength	62 N/mm^2	Radial shrinkage	3.7 %

PROPERTIES AND APPLICATIONS

This moderately heavy and sturdy wood has good physical properties, is very elastic and flexible, and is weather-resistant. It can be dried without much difficulty, but drying should be carried out slowly to prevent cracking. Freshly cut trunks should not be exposed to direct sunlight or warping may occur. Movingui is commonly used to produce panels, luxury flooring, and decorative veneers. It is also a versatile construction wood which is used, for example, to build timber frames for railroad cars and ships, as well as chemical storage boxes and laboratory tables.

USES
Indoor/Outdoor

Very Good	Good	Usable	Not Usable
flooring	construction wood	musical instruments	plywood
walls, decking	furniture	staircases	blind veneer
paneling	cabinetmaking	window frames	
intarsia works	doors	weapons industry	
laboratory furniture & fittings	ship, rail & truck building		
flat sawn veneer	rotary cut veneer		
	modeling		

MUBANGU *(Julbernardia sereti)*

Family: *Ceasalpiniaceae*

Other names: *Congo teak*
D.R. of the Congo: *mubangu, zebreli*
Cameroon: *ekop-beli*

HABITAT
Mubangu is found predominately in Cameroon and the Democratic Republic of the Congo; its habitat also extends to the coastal regions, where it is thinly distributed. The large quantities which exist in the eastern region of the Democratic Republic of the Congo are frequently found growing on ancient geological formations on the lower levels of the mountains. Settlements are often seen conspicuously near groups of mubangu as locals use the wood for indoor construction, furniture, and works of art.

TREE DESCRIPTION
The tree attains heights of up to 45 m (148 ft) with diameters between 60–100 cm (2–3.5 ft). The trunk can be branchless for up to 25 m (82 ft); it is straight and cylindrical, with a few root buttresses at the base.

WOOD DESCRIPTION
The sapwood is about 10 cm (4 in) thick. The core wood, which is not much differentiated from the sapwood, is yellowish-white to light-pink; after being felled the wood changes to a pinkish-copper color. It also has fine, dark stripes, 9–13 mm (.35–.5 in) wide, that lend beauty to the wood.

Durability Class	II	E – Module	14,300 N/mm^2
Raw density	0.77g/cm^3	Volume dwindle	15.0 %
Bending strength	145 N/mm^2	Tangential shrinkage	9.8 %
Compression strength	68 N/mm^2	Radial shrinkage	4.5 %

PROPERTIES AND APPLICATIONS

Mubangu is a moderately hard, fairly dense wood with good strength properties, above-average bending strength, and good flexibility. Its decorative grain makes it a good choice for veneers, flooring, and other ornamental applications. Thin rotary cut slices tend to get fungus spotting; to prevent this, the wood should be chemically treated prior to slicing. The veneer should be dried quickly after being cut.

USES

Indoor

Very Good	Good	Usable	Not Usable
flooring	furniture	construction wood	plywood
walls, decking	cabinetmaking	musical instruments	window frames
paneling	staircases	laboratory furniture & fittings	ship, rail & truck building
intarsia works	weapons industry		blind veneer
doors	rotary cut veneer		modeling
flat sawn veneer			

MUHIMBI *(Cynometra alexandri)*

Family:	*Caesalpiniaceae*
Other Names:	*mechindi*
Uganda:	*Uganda-ironwood, muhindi*
D.R. of the Congo:	*angu, baira, bapa, utuna, tembwe*

HABITAT
Muhimbi grows in the evergreen rain forests of the region around Lake Victoria and is particularly plentiful in Uganda. The tree, which grows well in dry sandy soil, is also found in savannah zones.

TREE DESCRIPTION
Muhimbi achieves heights of up to 45 m (148 ft) and diameters of 75–90 cm (2.5–3 ft). The trunks have large root buttresses that reduce the amount of usable timber to about a 12–15 m (39–49 ft) length. Younger trees grow straight, but older trees are frequently deformed and may contain a hollow or rotten core.

WOOD DESCRIPTION
The sapwood is up to 8 cm (3 in) thick. The core wood is normally reddish-brown with dark stripes, although color variations from violet to chestnut-brown are possible. The grain is irregular, and crystalline silicate deposits are often found in the pores.

Durability Class	I	**E – Module**	16,900 N/mm²
Raw density	1.20 g/cm³	**Volume dwindle**	12.0 %
Bending strength	162 N/mm²	**Tangential shrinkage**	6.5 %
Compression strength	68 N/mm²	**Radial shrinkage**	3.0 %

PROPERTIES AND APPLICATIONS

Muhimbi is very heavy and firm, and nearly impossible to bend. Slow kiln drying is recommended to avoid splintering and deformation. The wood is long-lived, weather resistant and impervious to insect attack. Its extreme hardness necessitates the usage of heavy-duty tools for processing. Muhimbi makes excellent flooring material and is frequently used to construct heavy ground floors (for example, the Royal Festival Hall in London). It is suitable for a variety of other interior and exterior construction projects.

USES
Indoor/Outdoor

Very Good	Good	Usable	Not Usable
flooring	construction wood	walls, decking	musical instruments
staircases	furniture	paneling	plywood
ship, rail & truck building	cabinetmaking	intarsia works	blind veneer
	doors	window frames	modeling
	laboratory furniture & fittings	rotary cut veneer	
	weapons industry		
	flat sawn veneer		

MUHUHU *(Brachylaena hutchinsii)*

Family: *Compositeae*

Other Names:
Kenya: *muhugwe, muhugu,*
                      mubuubu
Ethiopia: *karkarro*
Tanzania: *ol-magogo, watho*
Madagascar: *hazotokana*

HABITAT
Muhuhu is found in tropical East Africa, where it grows in dry regions and on mountains at altitudes of up to 1,800 m (5,906 ft). *Brachylaena ramiflora* and *Brachylaena merana* are two very rare sister species located in Madagascar.

TREE DESCRIPTION
Muhuhu is a medium-sized tree, up to 30 m (98 ft) tall and from 60–80 cm (2–2.5 ft) in diameter. The trunk, which is often twisted, is clear of branches up to 8 m (26 ft). Above-ground rootage is minimal.

WOOD DESCRIPTION
The thin sapwood is whitish- to brownish-yellow. The core wood is yellow-red to yellow-brown and has a distinctive multi-colored grain with beautiful stripes. In older trees the grain tends to be wavy.

Durability Class	I	E – Module	10,800 N/mm²
Raw density	0.85 – 0.95 g/cm³	Volume dwindle	9.3 %
Bending strength	122 N/mm²	Tangential shrinkage	5.6 %
Compression strength	67 N/mm²	Radial shrinkage	3.7 %

PROPERTIES AND APPLICATIONS

Muhuhu is a hard, heavy, durable wood; it is resistant to weather and insect attack. The drying process must be carried out very slowly and carefully since the wood can suffer wavy irregularities if dried too quickly. Among muhuhu's more common uses are the production of flooring, parquet, windows, doors, railway sleepers, and bridges.

USES
Indoor/Outdoor

Very Good	Good	Usable	Not Usable
	construction wood	paneling	intarsia works
	furniture	laboratory furniture & fittings	musical instruments
	flooring	modeling	plywood
	walls, decking		doors
	cabinetmaking		weapons industry
	staircases		rotary cut veneer
	window frames		flat sawn veneer
	ship, rail & truck building		blind veneer

MUKULUNGU *(Autranella congolensis)*

Family: *Sapotaceae*

Other Names: *kungulu*
Cameroon: *elang, elanzok*
Central African Rep.: *m'bamga, ovanga*
Rep. of the Congo: *m'fua*
D.R. of the Congo: *fino, kabulungu*
USA: *autracon*

HABITAT
This shade-loving tree is found in the humid forests of Central Africa. Its greatest concentrations exist in the Democratic Republic of the Congo, where on average, three to four of the trees are found per two acres.

TREE DESCRIPTION
Mukulungu is a large tree reaching heights of up to 40 m (131 ft) and diameters of 150–200 cm (5–6.5 ft) at chest height. Some specimens have been observed with diameters of 500 cm (16.5 ft). A large mukulungu tree can yield some 20 cubic meters (8,480 board feet) of timber. The trunk is straight and cylindrical, with the interesting characteristic of often displaying a slight thickening toward the top of the bole beneath the crown.

WOOD DESCRIPTION
The wood is a beautiful reddish-brown with dark veins; it occasionally has a light-purple or even multi-colored luster when viewed in well-lighted conditions. Mukulungu is fine-textured with a somewhat irregular grain.

Durability Class	I	E – Module	13,700 N/mm^2
Raw density	0.95 g/cm^3	Volume dwindle	20.0 %
Bending strength	150 N/mm^2	Tangential shrinkage	9.1 %
Compression strength	74 N/mm^2	Radial shrinkage	8.0 %

PROPERTIES AND APPLICATIONS

Mukulungu is a hard wood that has good mechanical properties and a superior bending strength. It is quite durable and weather- and water-resistant. Because of its extreme hardness, the wood can only be processed with special tools. Mukulungu is a good, though expensive, choice for uses such as staircases, windows and flooring. In past decades it was exported in great quantities to Europe, often being used to supply ceiling beams and construction timber for government buildings. The timber's high density and resistance to acids make it especially suitable for use in the manufacture of chemical containers and laboratory tables.

USES
Indoor/Outdoor

Very Good		Good	Usable	Not Usable
construction wood	laboratory furniture	musical instruments	ship, rail &	plywood
furniture	& fittings	window frames	truck building	blind veneer
flooring	weapons industry			modeling
walls, decking	rotary cut veneer			
paneling	flat sawn veneer			
intarsia works				
cabinetmaking				
doors				
staircases				

MUNINGA *(Pterocarpus angolensis)*

Family: *Papilionaceae*

Other Names: *Rhodesian walnut,*
brown-East-African
padouk
Mozambique: *umbila, imbila*
Zimbabwe: *mukwa, mutondo*
South Africa: *kiaat, transvaal-teak*
Tanzania: *mninga, kejuat*
Malawi: *mlombwa*
Angola: *mutete, girassonde*
D.R. of the Congo: *mutondo, mulombwa*

HABITAT
Muninga grows mainly in the dry, open forests of eastern and southern Africa where it is frequently found in mixed groups with umgusi (*Baikiaea plurijuga; see separate reference*). The tree is also found in tropical rain forests.

TREE DESCRIPTION
Muninga can attain heights of up to 25 m (82 ft) and diameters of 60–110 cm (2–3.5 ft). The trunk is cylindrical and free of branches for up to 10 m (33 ft). The bark is approximately 8 cm (3 in) thick and exudes a dark red resin when cut; for this reason the tree is sometimes referred to as bloodwood.

WOOD DESCRIPTION
Muninga is anatomically similar to all African padouk varieties. The yellow-brown core wood darkens upon exposure to a nut-brown color and has a beautiful wavy grain that is popular in the veneer industry. The sapwood is thin and whitish-yellow in color.

Durability Class	II	E – Module	13,000 N/mm^2
Raw density	0.65 – 0.80 g/cm^3	Volume dwindle	5.5 %
Bending strength	78 N/mm^2	Tangential shrinkage	2.7 %
Compression strength	65 N/mm^2	Radial shrinkage	2.2 %

PROPERTIES AND APPLICATIONS

Muninga is durable and weather- and insect-resistant. The wood dries slowly but well. It is used as construction timber, in shipbuilding, and in the plywood industry. In the veneer industry it is peeled and cut flat, often to produce decorative veneers for furniture.

USES

Indoor/Outdoor

Very Good	Good	Usable	Not Usable
construction wood	intarsia works	furniture	musical instruments
	cabinetmaking	flooring	
	staircases	walls, decking	
	ship, rail & truck building	paneling	
	rotary cut veneer	plywood	
	flat sawn veneer	doors	
		window frames	
		laboratory furniture & fittings	
		weapons industry	
		blind veneer	
		modeling	

MUSHARAGI / EAST AFRICAN OLIVE
(Olea hochstetteri)

Family: *Oleaceae*

Other Names: *East African olive*
Kenya: *muthat, ol-toliondo*
Tanzania: *murakoiwa,*
kiptateriondu
France: *musheragi*

HABITAT
Musharagi (also commonly known as East African olive) favors a reduced level of precipitation and consequently grows in mountainous regions at altitudes of some 2000–3000 m (6,562–9,843 ft). It is primarily found in the highlands of Kenya and Tanzania; additional locations include Uganda, Ethiopia and the eastern portion of the Democratic Republic of the Congo.

TREE DESCRIPTION
This is a rather small, often bush-like, tree that rarely reaches heights of more than 28 m (92 ft). Diameters ranging from 50–80 cm (1.5–2.5 ft) are typical, although specimens in Uganda and Ethiopia generally have smaller diameters of 30–50 cm (1–1.5 ft). The trunk yields on average about 10 m (33 ft) of branch-free, usable timber.

WOOD DESCRIPTION
The bright pink sapwood is up to 5 cm (2 in) thick. The core wood is oily and has a yellowish-orange color with gray-brown stripes and wavy lines. After cutting, the wood darkens.

Durability Class	II	E – Module	-
Raw density	0.90 g/cm³	Volume dwindle	-
Bending strength	107 N/mm²	Tangential shrinkage	10.0 %
Compression strength	75 N/mm²	Radial shrinkage	-

PROPERTIES AND APPLICATIONS

Musharagi is a hard, heavy wood whose good physical properties make it very stable; its durability, however, is only moderate, rendering it unsuitable for most outdoor applications. The wood has yet to be fully tested, so not all of its technical properties are known. The oil in the wood substantially elongates the drying process. Musharagi's decorative color variations and hardness make it a popular wood for interior fittings and solid wood flooring. It is a beautiful veneer wood, and its polished surfaces offer a particularly beautiful gloss; other uses include cabinetmaking and a variety of luxury products.

USES
Indoor

Very Good	Good	Usable	Not Usable
furniture	intarsia works	construction wood	plywood
flooring	staircases	musical instruments	blind veneer
walls, decking	weapons industry	doors	
paneling	rotary cut veneer	window frames	
cabinetmaking		laboratory furniture & fittings	
flat sawn veneer		ship, rail & truck building	
		modeling	

MUSIZI *(Maesopsis eminii)*

Family:	*Rhamnaceae*
Other Names:	*esenge, golden mahogany*
D.R. of the Congo:	*malingi*
Tanzania:	*muhunya, muhung*
Kenya:	*muhumula, mutere*
Ethiopia:	*buaywreng*
Liberia:	*awuru*
Ivory Coast:	*manasati*
Gabun:	*n'karle*

HABITAT

Musizi is a common tree species which grows in tropical deciduous forests across the breadth of Central Africa. It is often used to reforest grassy tracts of the savannah.

TREE DESCRIPTION

Musizi grows approximately 40 m (131 ft) high and has a diameter of 50–120 cm (1.5–4 ft); the trunk is clear of branches for up to 20 m (66 ft). The tree grows quickly but has a short life span.

WOOD DESCRIPTION

The white sapwood, which is some 6 cm (2.5 in) thick, has no useful applications. It is clearly demarcated from the yellowish core wood. After being cut and dried, the wood's color takes on the appearance of pure gold when exposed to bright light—thus it is occasionally referred to as the golden tree. The wood later darkens to gold-brown.

Durability Class	IV	**E – Module**	9,200 N/mm²
Raw density	0.40 – 0.50 g/cm³	**Volume dwindle**	9.0 %
Bending strength	75 N/mm²	**Tangential shrinkage**	10.0 %
Compression strength	46 N/mm²	**Radial shrinkage**	-

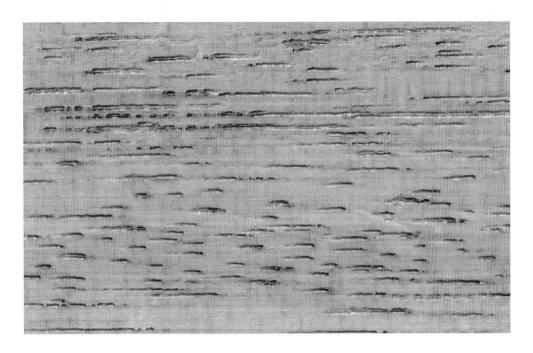

PROPERTIES AND APPLICATIONS

Musizi has long been used in the plywood industry and is considered a good alternative to European spruce, fir and pine. The wood is also frequently used to produce cheap decorative and blind veneers. Veneer slices must be quickly processed as they are susceptible to insects and humidity. Its golden color makes it a great intarsia wood. Musizia has been successfully used to produce paper pulp.

USES
Indoor

Very Good	Good	Usable	Not Usable
intarsia works	furniture		construction wood
plywood	walls, decking		flooring
rotary cut veneer	paneling		musical instruments
flat sawn veneer	cabinetmaking		doors
	blind veneer		staircases
	modeling		window frames
			laboratory furniture & fittings
			ship, rail & truck building
			weapons industry

MUSSIBI *(Guibourtia coleosperma)*

Family: *Caesalpiniaceae*

Other Names: *Rhodesian copalwood*
Zimbabwe: *musivi, omusivi, muxi*
Angola: *cuchibi, mehibi*
Namibia: *misibi, mosibi*
D.R. of the Congo: *mushi, mushibi*
Italy: *mogano de la Rhodesia*

HABITAT
Mussibi grows naturally in small groups in the dry forests of the southern half of Africa and is also cultivated in plantations. The tree is an important part of many local economies as its bark is used to make coloring materials, and the wood's oily secretions are mixed with water to produce an insect-repelling skin cream. Most exports come from Mozambique and Zimbabwe.

TREE DESCRIPTION
Mussibi is small in stature, between 12–20 m (39–66 ft) in height and 40–90 cm (1.5–3 ft) in diameter. The trunk is short, thick, and lumpy, yielding little usable timber.

WOOD DESCRIPTION
The white-gray sapwood is well-differentiated from the violet-red-brown core wood, which has dark narrow streaks. Both twisting growth patterns and the occasional irregular grain can create desirable decorative patterns. The wood is anatomically similar to bubinga (*Guibourtia tessmannii; see separate reference*).

Durability Class	II	E – Module	9,700 N/mm^2
Raw density	0.55 – 0.80 g/cm^3	Volume dwindle	-
Bending strength	90 N/mm^2	Tangential shrinkage	-
Compression strength	50 N/mm^2	Radial shrinkage	-

PROPERTIES AND APPLICATIONS

Mussibi is hard but workable, although it can splinter with nailing and should therefore be pre-drilled; also, its high resin content can cause saw blades to stick together. Mussibi is durable and can be used as an external building material. The wood takes glues well. Drying should be carefully controlled to prevent damage, and the wood should be well-steamed before being cut for veneers.

USES

Indoor/Outdoor

Very Good	Good	Usable	Not Usable
flat sawn veneer	construction wood	furniture	walls, decking
	flooring	paneling	intarsia works
	staircases	doors	musical instruments
	rotary cut veneer	window frames	cabinetmaking
		laboratory furniture & fittings	plywood
			ship, rail & truck building
			weapons industry
			blind veneer
			modeling

MUTENYE *(Guibourtia arnoldiana)*

Family:	*Caesalpiniaceae*
Other Names:	*olive walnut*
Cameroon:	*ogboneli, kouan*
Gabun:	*n'tene*
Rep. of the Congo:	*benge, libenge, tungi*
D.R. of the Congo:	*mutene*

HABITAT
The largest concentrations of mutenye are found in the damp evergreen tropical forests of the central Congo basin, in Cameroon, and in Cabinda. The tree prefers humid forest soils.

TREE DESCRIPTION
Mutenye is a medium-sized tree; it can attain heights of up to 25 m (82 ft) and diameters of 60–90 cm (2–3 ft). The trunk is cylindrical and clear of branches for 10–15 m (33–49 ft). Small root buttresses are often present.

WOOD DESCRIPTION
The white-gray sapwood differs clearly from the core wood, which is yellow- to walnut-brown with dark brown-black stripes. Numerous resin channels may be present which give the wood, when freshly cut, an unpleasant smell.

Durability Class	II	**E – Module**	15,500 N/mm²
Raw density	0.82 g/cm³	**Volume dwindle**	13.0 %
Bending strength	150 N/mm²	**Tangential shrinkage**	8.5 %
Compression strength	80 N/mm²	**Radial shrinkage**	4.7 %

PROPERTIES AND APPLICATIONS

This heavy, medium-hard wood possesses good static physical properties, although it dynamic properties are only average. Drying must be slowly and carefully executed to prevent tears in the wood. Mutenye is durable and, after drying, also weather- and insect-resistant. In the veneer industry mutenye is peeled and cut flat; it is often used to produce beautiful decorative finishes. It is also used to construct stairs and flooring. More time is needed before the timber's best uses in the furniture industry are known, although it has already proven itself for solid-wood projects.

USES
Indoor/Outdoor

Very Good	Good	Usable	Not Usable
	furniture	modeling	construction wood
	flooring		plywood
	walls, decking		laboratory furniture & fittings
	paneling		ship, rail & truck building
	intarsia works		weapons industry
	musical instruments		blind veneer
	cabinetmaking		
	doors		
	staircases		
	window frames		
	rotary cut veneer		
	flat sawn veneer		

MUYATI *(Mildbraediodendron excelsum)*

Family: *Caesalpiniaceae*

Other Names:
D.R. of the Congo: *andrata*

HABITAT
The largely unknown muyati, whose botanical designation was only recently assigned, grows in the damp evergreen forests of the Ituri region in the Democratic Republic of the Congo.

TREE DESCRIPTION
Muyati is a medium-sized tree some 40 m (131 ft) tall and 70–90 cm (2.5–3 ft) in diameter. The trunk is straight and cylindrical, with 25–30 m (82–98 ft) of branchless, usable timber. Root buttresses are insignificant.

WOOD DESCRIPTION
The yellow-brown sapwood is up to 10 cm (4 in) thick. The core wood is dark-brown with an irregular grain, similar to tali (*Erythrophleum suaveolens; see separate reference*).

Durability Class	III	**E – Module**	12,500 N/mm²
Raw density	0.76 g/cm³	**Volume dwindle**	10.5 %
Bending strength	126 N/mm²	**Tangential shrinkage**	-
Compression strength	60 N/mm²	**Radial shrinkage**	-

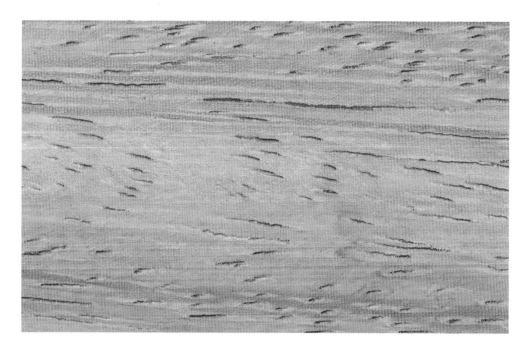

PROPERTIES AND APPLICATIONS

Muyati is a heavy, stable wood that is resistant to both the weather and insect attack. Despite its hardness, it has good elasticity. Not much is known of muyati and much technical testing remains to be done. However, early observations indicate it is suitable for flooring and construction projects, as well as for various applications in the furniture industry and for the building of external decking, stairs, doors and panels. Also, the wood's unusual oblong grain can create beautiful veneer patterns.

USES

Indoor/Outdoor

Very Good	Good	Usable	Not Usable
	furniture	construction wood	musical instruments
	flooring	paneling	plywood
	walls, decking	intarsia works	blind veneer
	cabinetmaking	laboratory furniture & fittings	modeling
	doors	ship, rail & truck building	
	staircases	weapons industry	
	window frames		
	rotary cut veneer		
	flat sawn veneer		

NAGA *(Brachystegia cynometroides)*

Family:	*Caesalpiniaceae*
Other Names:	*okwen, rayona*
Cameroon:	*ekop, tebako*

HABITAT
Naga grows in close groups in the damp evergreen forests of Cameroon. In the old secondary forests, the trees are more scattered.

TREE DESCRIPTION
Naga has a short trunk and root buttresses up to 4 m (13 ft) high. It is between 80–120 cm (2.5–4 ft) in diameter. Young and old naga trees can be differentiated by the coloration of their bark: the bark of younger trees is white yellow, while that of older trees is orange-red.

WOOD DESCRIPTION
The white-brown-pink sapwood is between 5–15 cm (2–6 in) thick. The core wood is ochre-brown to copper-brown-violet; it has a sometimes irregular grain and narrow light and dark stripes. Resin channels may be present.

Durability Class	III	E – Module	15,400 N/mm²
Raw density	0.76 g/cm³	Volume dwindle	13.7 %
Bending strength	117 N/mm²	Tangential shrinkage	8.9 %
Compression strength	72 N/mm²	Radial shrinkage	4.8 %

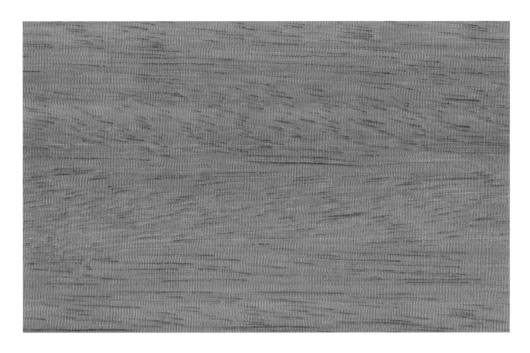

PROPERTIES AND APPLICATIONS

This rough, fibrous wood structurally resembles sapelli (*Entandrophragma cylindricum; see separate reference*). It has good physical properties, is durable, and is also weather- and insect-resistant. The wood should be treated with a preservative immediately after cutting to prevent cracking. The drying process should be carried out carefully and slowly as the wood is otherwise liable to tear. Naga is used for the production of windows, doors, floors, stairs, and also as veneer wood.

USES
Indoor/Outdoor

Very Good	Good	Usable	Not Usable
	flooring	construction wood	intarsia works
	walls, decking	furniture	musical instruments
	doors	paneling	
	staircases	cabinetmaking	
	window frames	plywood	
	rotary cut veneer	laboratory furniture & fittings	
	flat sawn veneer	ship, rail & truck building	
		weapons industry	
		blind veneer	
		modeling	

NIANGON *(Heritiera utilis)*

Family:	*Sterculiaceae*	

Other Names: *niangon, cola-mahahoni*
Ghana: *attabini, niankuma*
Ivory Coast: *kouanda, yangon*
Gabun: *ogoue, akevau,*
engongkom
Liberia: *wishmore, kekosi*
Germany: *angi*

HABITAT
Niangon grows in the damp tropical evergreen forests of West Africa, preferring coastal and riverbank areas. Its primary habitat extends from Liberia in the west to the Democratic Republic of the Congo in the east. This tree can be found growing in particularly large groups in Ivory Coast and Ghana.

TREE DESCRIPTION
Niangon is a medium-sized tree that can be up to 40 m (131 ft) in height and 50–100 cm (1.5–3.5 ft) in diameter. Specimens growing in drier areas have straight and cylindrical trunks; however those found in damper areas tend to have a bent stature. In either case the trunk can be branch-free for up to 20 m (66 ft).

WOOD DESCRIPTION
The white-gray sapwood is approximately 5 cm (2 in) thick. The core wood is yellowish- to violet-brown with narrow brown stripes, is greasy and dull, and has crystalline deposits of calcium oxalate. The fibers are typically straight and of varying thickness. On occasion the grain has a wavy appearance.

Durability Class	II	E – Module	11,500 N/mm²
Raw density	0.64 g/cm³	Volume dwindle	13.0 %
Bending strength	105 N/mm²	Tangential shrinkage	8.5 %
Compression strength	55 N/mm²	Radial shrinkage	3.8 %

PROPERTIES AND APPLICATIONS

This medium-hard and moderately-heavy wood has good physical properties and is very impact- and pressure-resistant. It can be dried, cut and processed without much difficulty. In most applications, no preservative treatment is required. When steamed the wood has a high resin output. Niangon's durability makes it suitable for outdoor construction. It is also used for stairs, floors, windows and doors.

USES

Indoor/Outdoor

Very Good	Good	Usable	Not Usable
doors	construction wood	walls, decking	furniture
staircases	flooring	paneling	musical instruments
window frames	rotary cut veneer	intarsia works	plywood
	flat sawn veneer	cabinetmaking	laboratory furniture & fittings
		ship, rail & truck building	blind veneer
		weapons industry	modeling

NIOVE *(Staudtia stipitata)*

Family:	*Myristicaceae*

Other Names:	*niove*
Cameroon:	*ekop, bope, n'bonda*
Guinea-Bissau:	*menga-menga*
Gabon:	*ohobe, m'boune, m'bou*
Rep. of the Congo:	*bosasa, kamashi*
D.R. of the Congo:	*susumenga*
Angola:	*memenga*

HABITAT
Niove grows in evergreen forests throughout tropical West Africa. The largest concentrations exist in Cameroon, where the tree is frequently found in large groups.

TREE DESCRIPTION
This medium-sized species can attain a height of 35 m (115 ft) and diameters of 70–100 cm (2.5–3.5 ft). The trunk grows very straight and cylindrically and is clear of branches up to 20 m (66 ft); it is not buttressed. The wood may secrete a red latex juice when cut.

WOOD DESCRIPTION
The white-yellow to pink sapwood is approximately 4 cm (1.5 in) thick. The core wood is ochre-red to orange-brown, usually with dark stripes. Fresh niove wood smells like pepper. After a lengthy period of storage, a white-blue lining may appear in the wood's radial plane.

Durability Class	II	**E – Module**	15,000 N/mm²
Raw density	0.89 – 1.05 g/cm³	**Volume dwindle**	11.8 %
Bending strength	160 N/mm²	**Tangential shrinkage**	6.4 %
Compression strength	85 N/mm²	**Radial shrinkage**	5.1 %

PROPERTIES AND APPLICATIONS

Niove is a very hard and heavy wood with an even structure and good physical properties; it is, however, impact-sensitive. The timber's high resin content contributes to its high level of durability. The drying process must be carefully controlled and slowly performed. If well-steamed, niove is suitable for veneer production. It is a good general construction wood, usable for both interior and exterior purposes. Common applications include the building of stairs, doors and floors.

USES

Indoor/Outdoor

Very Good	Good	Usable	Not Usable
	construction wood	furniture	intarsia works
	flooring	cabinetmaking	musical instruments
	walls, decking	doors	plywood
	paneling	window frames	laboratory furniture & fittings
	staircases	rotary cut veneer	weapons industry
	ship, rail & truck building	flat sawn veneer	blind veneer
			modeling

OBECHE / ABACHI *(Triplochiton scleroxylon)*

Family: *Sterculiaceae*

Other Names: *abachi, ayous,*
African maple
Ivory Coast: *samba*
Ghana: *wawa*
D.R. of the Congo: *arere, nkom*
Central African Rep.: *ayous, ayus*

HABITAT
Obeche grows in damp evergreen forests and is a common tree in much of West Africa. In Ghana it is called wawa, and it is referred to as ayous in Cameroon, the Central African Republic, and Equatorial Guinea.

TREE DESCRIPTION
Obeche is a stately tree that grows to about 40 m (131 ft) in height and is between 60–90 cm (2–3 ft) in diameter, with the specimens in Ghana tending to be somewhat thicker. It has very high (up to 8 m (26 ft)) and irregularly-shaped root buttresses; otherwise the trunk is straight and clear of branches for up to 25 m (82 ft).

WOOD DESCRIPTION
The sapwood and core wood, which are hardly differentiated, are almost white to yellowish-white in color; occasionally the core wood has a yellow-olive-brown hue, and specimens in Cameroon tend to have a golden-yellow luster. The wood has an even grain.

Durability Class	III	E – Module	6,000 N/mm^2
Raw density	0.40 g/cm^3	Volume dwindle	9.1 %
Bending strength	73 N/mm^2	Tangential shrinkage	5.6 %
Compression strength	30 N/mm^2	Radial shrinkage	3.3 %

PROPERTIES AND APPLICATIONS

Obeche is a light wood, but with average physical properties and good elasticity. In relation to its weight, it is very stable, flexible and shock-resistant. It is well-suited for producing rotary cut and flat sawn veneers, and fresh wood is sufficiently soft to be peeled without being steamed. Obeche can be used to provide both solid-wood and blind veneer components for door production. It is also used in the furniture industry, for the making of organs and pianos, for aircraft construction, and for cabinetmaking.

USES
Indoor

Very Good	Good	Usable	Not Usable
rotary cut veneer	furniture	construction wood	intarsia works
flat sawn veneer	musical instruments	flooring	
blind veneer	cabinetmaking	walls, decking	
	doors	paneling	
	staircases	plywood	
	modeling	window frames	
		laboratory furniture & fittings	
		ship, rail & truck building	
		weapons industry	

OBOTO *(Mammea africana)*

Family:	*Guttiferen-Clusiaceae*

Other Names:

D.R. of the Congo:	*boza, eteya, tschilunga, mamea, m'bossi*
Ivory Coast:	*djimbo*
Ghana:	*passee*
Nigeria:	*ukutu*
Cameroon:	*abotzok*
Gabon:	*bokoli*

HABITAT
Oboto's zone of distribution extends from Sierra Leone along the Gulf of Guinea coast to Cabinda and Angola, and east reaching the Congo basin, where the stocks are particularly lush. It thrives in humid evergreen forest environments.

TREE DESCRIPTION
Oboto grows up to 30 m (98 ft) high. The very straight and cylindrical trunk has a diameter of 80–100 cm (2.5–3.5 ft) and is normally free of branches to a height of about 20 m (66 ft). There are frequently thick and gnarled roots climbing up the tree. The timber yield of an Oboto trunk is variable but often rather small.

WOOD DESCRIPTION
The pink to reddish-brown core wood is demarcated from the light pink sapwood, which can be up to 6 cm (2.5 in) thick. After being felled, the wood darkens considerably and displays a deep, dark red color similar to mahogany with a light violet tone. Many pieces have dark oily spots.

Durability Class	II	E – Module	~ 12,500 N/mm^2
Raw density	0.67 – 0.86 g/cm^3	Volume dwindle	~ 16.0 %
Bending strength	~ 127 N/mm^2	Tangential shrinkage	10.0 %
Compression strength	~ 65 N/mm^2	Radial shrinkage	6.5 %

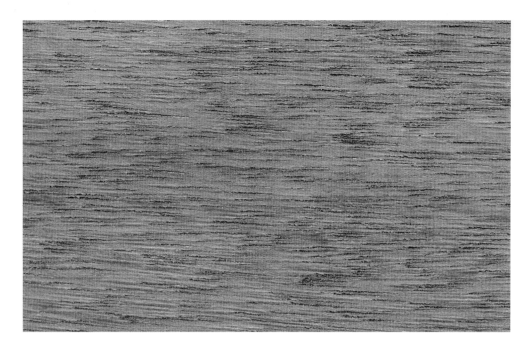

PROPERTIES AND APPLICATIONS

Oboto is a medium-hard, moderately heavy wood. It is elastic, has good shock resistance, and is quite workable overall. The timber's high moisture content gives it a strong tendency to crack, so the drying process must be carefully executed. The wood is suitable for exterior and interior carpentry, such as flooring, staircases, and posts. It is also used to produce laboratory and acid containers because of its resistance to acids. Further uses include bridge and ship construction.

USES
Indoor/Outdoor

Very Good	Good	Usable	Not Usable
paneling	construction wood		musical instruments
intarsia works	furniture		plywood
staircases	flooring		blind veneer
	walls, decking		modeling
	cabinetmaking		
	doors		
	window frames		
	laboratory furniture & fittings		
	ship, rail & truck building		
	weapons industry		
	rotary cut veneer		
	flat sawn veneer		

OHIA *(Celtis soyauxii)*

Family:	*Ulmaceae*

Other Names:

Ivory Coast:	*lohofne, ba, koasan, asan*
Nigeria:	*hako, ita*
Congo countries:	*lumiumbu, bolunde, kayombo*

HABITAT

Ohia is widely distributed in deciduous forests across Central Africa. It grows well in the drier environments of higher elevations; for example, the tree is common in the Lake Victoria region where it grows at altitudes of up to 1,700 m (5,577 ft) above sea level. Usually no more than five to ten specimens are found per acre of forest.

TREE DESCRIPTION

The ohia tree can reach a height of 30–40 m (98–131 ft). The trunk is mostly straight and cylindrical; there are root buttresses at the base, some rather extensive and extending upwards some 6 m (20 ft). The tree has a relatively small crown, a typical diameter of about 80 cm (2.5 ft), and can be branchless to 25 m (82 ft).

WOOD DESCRIPTION

The yellowish-white sapwood is barely distinguishable from the pale-yellowish core wood. After felling, the core wood gradually becomes gray-white in color. Most cut surfaces will evidence a beautiful satin-like gleam, in addition to decorative, wavy stripes on the cross section. The wood has very regular, even pores and fine fibers.

Durability Class	III	**E – Module**	13,500 N/mm²
Raw density	0.70 – 0.80 g/cm³	**Volume dwindle**	12.8 %
Bending strength	130 N/mm²	**Tangential shrinkage**	8.9 %
Compression strength	59 N/mm²	**Radial shrinkage**	5.0 %

PROPERTIES AND APPLICATIONS

Ohia is a medium-hard to very hard wood with good strength properties but has suspect flexibility and an appreciable tendency to crack. Despite its moderate durability, ohia has been successfully applied to a wide range of uses, including the manufacturing of sports equipment, boxes, marine support beams (for docks and such) and trucks. High-quality logs are processed, after a thorough chemical treatment, into flooring; ohia's high level of resistance to wear and tear in fact makes it a good choice for heavy-duty floors. In England it is used as a replacement for maple in dancing floors because of its beautiful natural coloring.

USES

Indoor

Very Good	Good	Usable	Not Usable
	flooring	furniture	construction wood
	walls, decking	paneling	musical instruments
	ship, rail & truck building	intarsia works	plywood
		cabinetmaking	window frames
		doors	laboratory furniture & fittings
		staircases	weapons industry
		flat sawn veneer	rotary cut veneer
			blind veneer
			modeling

OKAN / DENYA *(Cylicodiscus gabunensis)*

Family:	*Mimosaceae*

Other Names: *denya*
Ghana: *denya, adadua*
Ivory Coast: *bouemon*
Gabon: *edum, oduma*
Cameroon: *adoum, bokoka*
Nigeria: *anyan, ekam, okain, kendum*

HABITAT
Okan is an abundant wood growing in the evergreen rain forests of West Africa. Its habitat extends from Sierra Leone in the west to Gabon in the south. The people of southern Nigeria consider the tree to be holy.

TREE DESCRIPTION
This species is one of the largest trees in Africa; it reaches imposing heights of 40–60 m (131–197 ft), with diameters of 200 cm (6.5 ft) or more. The trunk is straight, cylindrical, and free of branches up to 35 m (115 ft). The crown is quite pronounced.

WOOD DESCRIPTION
The sapwood is white-pink and up to 8 cm (3 in) thick; in older trees the sapwood is thinner and white-green. The color of the core wood varies from yellow-brown to dark red-brown, and slim dark stripes add a beautiful dimension to the grain. The wood develops a gold-yellow gleam after air-drying.

Durability Class	I	E – Module	15,000–18,000 N/mm^2
Raw density	0.77 – 1.05 g/cm^3	Volume dwindle	14.5 %
Bending strength	150 N/mm^2	Tangential shrinkage	8.6 %
Compression strength	85 N/mm^2	Radial shrinkage	6.2 %

PROPERTIES AND APPLICATIONS
This hard and heavy wood possesses good mechanical properties. Kiln drying must be carried out slowly and carefully or the wood can become spotted. It resists weather and insect attack and is used as heavy construction timber for, among other things, the building of bridges and the manufacturing of railway sleepers and heavy floors. In parts of Nigeria okan is used to make pontoons.

USES
Indoor/Outdoor

Very Good	Good	Usable	Not Usable
construction wood	flooring	walls, decking	furniture
ship, rail & truck building			paneling
			intarsia works
			musical instruments
			cabinetmaking
			plywood
			doors
			staircases
			window frames
			laboratory furniture & fittings
			weapons industry
			rotary cut veneer
			flat sawn veneer
			blind veneer
			modeling

OKOUME *(Aucoumea klaineana)*

Family: *Burseraceae*

Other Names: *okoume, gaboon*
Equatorial-Guinea: *mofoumon, n'ggoumi, n'koumi, zonga*
Gabon: *angouma*

HABITAT
Okoume (also commonly known as gaboon) grows predominately in Gabon and Equatorial Guinea. Okoume comprises some 60 percent of the trees in the forests of Gabon. The tree is also found in southern Cameroon and in the two Congo states, but these stocks are not of commercial interest due to their small quantity.

TREE DESCRIPTION
Okoume, which can reach a height of 40 m (131 ft), is typically topped with a spherical crown. Trunk diameters vary between 60–180 cm (2–6 ft). The bole is cylindrical and clear of branches up to 35 m (115 ft), with large root buttresses that can grow up to 3 m (10 ft) high.

WOOD DESCRIPTION
The white-gray sapwood, up to 10 cm (4 in) thick, can constitute up to 15 percent of the wood. The core wood is usually a dark, even pink color, although occasionally it is reddish-brown. Special characteristics of this wood include its silky sheen and numerous thin dark stripes.

Durability Class	III	E – Module	15,000–18,000 N/mm^2
Raw density	0.38 – 0.55g/cm^3	Volume dwindle	14.5 %
Bending strength	80 N/mm^2	Tangential shrinkage	8.6 %
Compression strength	38 N/mm^2	Radial shrinkage	6.2 %

PROPERTIES AND APPLICATIONS

Okoume is a lighter wood, not dissimilar from pine and beech. It has a medium level of firmness, can be dried well, and is resistant to insects but not weather. The wood can be easily processed; however sawing should be done with hard metal-alloy blades to compensate for the presence of crystalline deposits. Okoume makes an ideal veneer wood and is also used in the furniture and plywood industries, and for the production of paper pulp and cigar boxes. With appropriate chemical treatments, the timber can also be used as temporary engineering support wood for water-based construction projects.

USES
Indoor

Very Good	Good	Usable	Not Usable
furniture	paneling	construction wood	intarsia works
plywood	cabinetmaking	flooring	staircases
rotary cut veneer		walls, decking	window frames
flat sawn veneer		musical instruments	laboratory furniture & fittings
blind veneer		doors	weapons industry
modeling		ship, rail & truck building	

OLONVOGO *(Fagara macrophylla)*

Family:	*Rutaceae*
Other Names:	*olon, white African mahogany*
Ivory Coast:	*hangwa, bahe*
Ghana:	*yea*
Nigeria:	*uko, atogbo, okor*
Cameroon:	*bongo*
D.R. of the Congo:	*kasambumba*

HABITAT
Olonvogo is concentrated in humid tropical forests in Ivory Coast, Cameroon, Equatorial Guinea, Gabon and the Democratic Republic of the Congo.

TREE DESCRIPTION
The tree reaches heights of no more than 30 m (98 ft), with diameters typically varying between 40–90 cm (1.5–3 ft). The trunk is mostly straight and cylindrical, branchless up to 20 m (66 ft), and frequently displaying wart-like deformities that end in thin, thorn-like tips.

WOOD DESCRIPTION
The thin, yellow-white sapwood differs only marginally from the core wood, which is yellow to grayish-green and shines like silk on all cut planes. The pores are not very numerous, appearing singly or in pairs and reaching a size of 4 to 6 square millimeters. Freshly cut wood has a strong, sweet smell.

Durability Class	II	**E – Module**	-
Raw density	0.75 – 0.85 g/cm³	**Volume dwindle**	14.9 %
Bending strength	148 – 176 N/mm²	**Tangential shrinkage**	8.7 %
Compression strength	82 N/mm²	**Radial shrinkage**	-

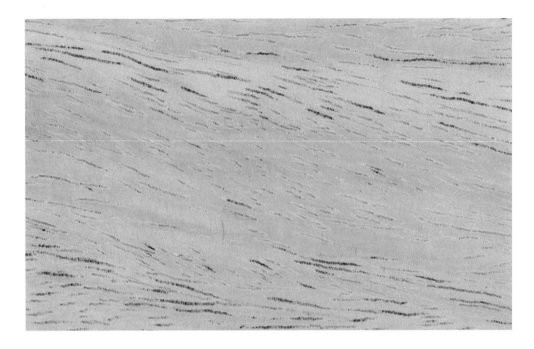

PROPERTIES AND APPLICATIONS

This hard, heavy wood is durable and possesses good mechanical strength properties which are, in part, superior to those of European oak. Its bending strength is outstanding, and the wood is extremely workable when steamed. Kiln drying is a trouble-free process as the wood rarely cracks or inclines. Olonvogo accepts stable bolt and glue connections, making it highly suitable for heavy construction projects. Common applications include boat and wagon construction. Carpenters use this wood to make furniture, interior works, paneling, and ceiling veneers, and it is highly popular in the plywood industry.

USES
Indoor

Very Good	Good	Usable	Not Usable
flooring	construction wood	furniture	musical instruments
	walls, decking	staircases	plywood
	paneling	window frames	laboratory furniture & fittings
	intarsia works	weapons industry	blind veneer
	cabinetmaking	rotary cut veneer	modeling
	doors		
	ship, rail & truck building		
	flat sawn veneer		

ONZABILI *(Antrocaryon klaineanum)*

Family:	*Anacardiaceae*
Other Names:	*bibolo, dark limba*
Cameroon:	*bougongi, diolo, engongui, ombega*
D.R. of the Congo:	*angolo mongongo*
Ghana:	*ekio, akoua*

HABITAT
Onzabili is found in the tropical regions of Africa, where it is often called bibolo. It was first identified in Gabon in 1898. The *Antrocaryon* species, including this one, are similar to kumbi (*Lannea welwitschii; see separate reference*), the other member of this family which offers usable wood.

TREE DESCRIPTION
This tree achieves heights of up to 50 m (164 ft), with diameters between 50–80 cm (1.5–2.5 ft). The trunks are even and cylindrical, often with groove-like imprints, and can be clear of branches up to 30 m (98 ft).

WOOD DESCRIPTION
Sapwood and core wood hardly differ in appearance; the core wood is rather rough and white-pink to red yellow-brown in color. Cut planes often have a mother-of-pearl-like gloss. Freshly-sawed wood resembles khaya (*Khaya anthotheca; see separate reference*) or okoume (*Aucoumea klaineana; see separate reference*).

Durability Class	II	**E – Module**	10,500 N/mm²
Raw density	0.66 – 0.80 g/cm³	**Volume dwindle**	13.3 %
Bending strength	115 N/mm²	**Tangential shrinkage**	6.8 %
Compression strength	53 N/mm²	**Radial shrinkage**	4.3 %

PROPERTIES AND APPLICATIONS

This moderately heavy but soft wood has generally good physical properties. It is, however, not weatherproof and is very susceptible to insect attack (particularly from the wood drilling beetle [*Apate monachus*]). The wood must be chemically treated prior to shipment. Onzabili is a good wood for rotary cut veneers used in plywood production. It also has interior carpentry applications and has been found useful for modeling.

USES

Indoor

Very Good	Good	Usable	Not Usable
plywood	rotary cut veneer	construction wood	flooring
blind veneer	modeling	furniture	intarsia works
		walls, decking	musical instruments
		paneling	cabinetmaking
		flat sawn veneer	doors
			staircases
			window frames
			laboratory furniture & fittings
			ship, rail & truck building
			weapons industry

OVENGKOL *(Guibourtia ehie)*

Family:	*Caesalpiniaceae*
Other Names:	*mongoinuss*
Equatorial Guinea:	*ovangkol, mongoy,*
	palissandro
Ivory Coast:	*amazakoue*
Ghana:	*hyedua, anokye*
Nigeria:	*kaluk*

HABITAT

The rare ovengkol tends to grow alone from others of its kind; it is found in the Congo basin, western Uganda, and in some countries bordering the Gulf of Guinea. Two new *Guibourtia* species were discovered in recent years, so there is much yet to learn about the genus.

TREE DESCRIPTION

This approximately 30 m (98 ft) tall tree achieves a diameter of only about 50 cm (1.5 ft). The trunk is straight and cylindrical and buttressed to a height of about 2 m (7 ft).

WOOD DESCRIPTION

The clearly demarcated sapwood is about 8 cm (3 in) thick and has a white-yellow color. The core wood is largely yellowish- to blackish-brown, but a more intense and commercially valuable gray-violet coloration, with black stripes, may be present in the center. The pores contain a wax-like substance.

Durability Class	III	E – Module	14,000 N/mm²
Raw density	0.75 – 0.85 g/cm³	Volume dwindle	13.3 %
Bending strength	145 N/mm²	Tangential shrinkage	8.0 %
Compression strength	70 N/mm²	Radial shrinkage	4.2 %

PROPERTIES AND APPLICATIONS

Ovengkol is a hard, straight-growing wood—it dries easily, is moderately durable, and is resistant to insect attack. It is a particularly desirable choice for flat sawn veneers, and its salient grain makes it popular in the furniture and cabinetmaking industries. Ovengkol is often used as a substitute for pallisandre when pallisandre is unavailable.

USES

Indoor

Very Good	Good	Usable	Not Usable
	furniture	construction wood	musical instruments
	intarsia works	flooring	plywood
	cabinetmaking	walls, decking	staircases
	rotary cut veneer	paneling	window frames
	flat sawn veneer	doors	laboratory furniture & fittings
		weapons industry	ship, rail & truck building
			blind veneer
			modeling

PADOUK *(Pterocarpus soyauxii)*

Family:	*Fabaceae*
Other Names:	*African padouk, barwood*
Nigeria:	*osun*
Cameroon:	*mbe, issigou, muenge*
Congo countries:	*kisese, tukula, nzali*
Angola:	*tukala*
Tanzania:	*mwangura*

HABITAT
The African padouk tree grows in the damp evergreen forests of Central Africa, from Nigeria in the west to Angola in the south. In Gabon and Cameroon it is found growing individually, but nevertheless very numerously.

TREE DESCRIPTION
Padouk trees attain a height of nearly 40 m (131 ft) with a maximum diameter of 100–120 cm (3.5–4 ft). The trunks are topped by a small crown and have high, thin root buttresses. Usually about 20 m (66 ft) of the bole is branch-free, yielding some 20 cubic meters (8476 board ft) of usable timber.

WOOD DESCRIPTION
The yellowish-white sapwood, up to 20 cm (8 in) thick, is totally useless. Freshly-cut core wood is bright red in color, and later darkens to orange or reddish-brown. Cut planes may display beautiful decorative stripes and multi-colored patterns, often filled with reddish, crystalline content.

Durability Class	II	E – Module	12,300 N/mm²
Raw density	0.77 g/cm³	Volume dwindle	9.0 %
Bending strength	131 N/mm²	Tangential shrinkage	5.3 %
Compression strength	62 N/mm²	Radial shrinkage	3.3 %

PROPERTIES AND APPLICATIONS

Padouk is flexible and impact-resistant. It is very workable, and drying results in little shrinkage or twisting (although kiln drying may produce a few small breaks). After cutting, the wood should be quickly processed as it loses some of its vibrant coloring if stored for too long. Padouk is a first-class flat sawn veneer wood, and is ideal for intarsia works, for the cabinetmaker and for musical instruments. Its outstanding longevity and physical properties make it useful for applications such flooring and paneling. It is also sought after for the making of musical instruments.

USES
Indoor/Outdoor

Very Good	Good	Usable	Not Usable
furniture	flooring	construction wood	plywood
intarsia works	walls, decking	staircases	blind veneer
musical instruments	paneling	window frames	
cabinetmaking	doors	laboratory furniture	
weapons industry	rotary cut veneer	& fittings	
flat sawn veneer		ship, rail & truck building	
modeling			

PANGA PANGA *(Millettia stuhlmannii)*

Family:	*Fabaceae*
Other Names:	*jambire*
Mozambique:	*jambire*
Tanzania:	*mpande, partidge wood*

HABITAT
Panga panga grows in the damp evergreen tropical forests of East Africa. The largest concentrations are found in Mozambique; sparser populations exist in southern Tanzania.

TREE DESCRIPTION
The tree can grow to a height of up to 20 m (66 ft) with diameters ranging from 40–80 cm (1.5–2.5 ft). The trunk rarely grows straight; the bark is thin and light yellow in color.

WOOD DESCRIPTION
The dark- to black-brown core wood is clearly differentiated from the yellowish, approximately 5 cm (2 in) thick, sapwood. A series of light and dark layers give the wood a notable and very decorative appearance. Panga panga is often erroneously sold as wenge (*Millettia laurenti; see separate reference*), a similar tree from the same family (wenge is more darkly colored).

Durability Class	I	**E – Module**	13,700 N/mm²
Raw density	0.78 – 0.82 g/cm³	**Volume dwindle**	9.0 %
Bending strength	120 N/mm²	**Tangential shrinkage**	5.6 %
Compression strength	68 N/mm²	**Radial shrinkage**	3.0 %

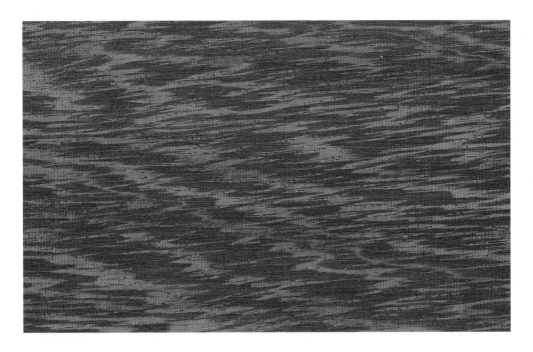

PROPERTIES AND APPLICATIONS

Panga panga is a very hard and heavy wood; it possesses good mechanical and physical properties, and is flexible, durable, and weather- and insect-resistant. Kiln drying should be undertaken in a slow fashion in order to reduce the incidence of cracking. The wood glues poorly, although this condition may be ameliorated by first filling up the pores. Panga panga is very popular in the veneer industry, where it is used for decorative furniture. Intensive steaming must be performed prior to veneer processing. The wood's durability and optical elegance make it a good, if somewhat costly, solution for flooring needs. Because of its high price, panga panga is no longer used as construction timber.

USES
Indoor/Outdoor

Very Good	Good	Usable	Not Usable
furniture	walls, decking	construction wood	plywood
flooring	paneling	musical instruments	ship, rail & truck building
rotary cut veneer	intarsia works	window frames	blind veneer
flat sawn veneer	cabinetmaking	laboratory furniture & fittings	modeling
	doors		
	staircases		
	weapons industry		

PAO ROSA *(Swartzia fistuloides)*

Family:	*Ceasalpiniaceae*

Other Names: *amaranth*
Ivory Coast: *boto*
Cameroon: *bata*
Gabon: *oken, dina*
Congo countries: *kiela kusu*
Brazil: *pao roxo*

HABITAT
Pao rosa grows mainly at the equatorial region of West-Central Africa, including the countries of Cameroon, Gabon, and the Republic of the Congo. At present, no other substantial habitat zones are known, although the species has on occasion been observed in East Africa. Other *Swartzia* varieties can be found in South America.

TREE DESCRIPTION
Pao rosa achieves a maximum height of 30 m (98 ft) with a diameter of 50–90 cm (1.5–3 ft). The trunk is usually irregular and inclined. The tree produces a bean-like fruit.

WOOD DESCRIPTION
The white-yellow to white-pink sapwood is clearly demarcated from the pink-red-violet core wood. Narrow, dark red stripes are present; these fade, however, during exposure to light. The bark discharges a red-violet resin.

Durability Class	II	**E – Module**	17,000 N/mm^2
Raw density	1.05 g/cm^3	**Volume dwindle**	13.5 %
Bending strength	166 N/mm^2	**Tangential shrinkage**	6.2 %
Compression strength	90 N/mm^2	**Radial shrinkage**	4.4 %

PROPERTIES AND APPLICATIONS

Pao rosa wood is hard and heavy, with good mechanical and physical properties. It has good compression and bending strengths, and is flexible and durable. Although the wood is weather resistant, it is best suited for indoors applications. The drying process is very lengthy; the wood should be well-steamed before being veneer-processed. Pao rosa is commonly used as a veneer wood and, in the furniture industry, serves as a replacement for palissandre. To date the wood has seen little exposure in Europe and North America.

USES
Indoor

Very Good	Good	Usable	Not Usable
flat sawn veneer	furniture	modeling	construction wood
	flooring		musical instruments
	walls, decking		plywood
	paneling		doors
	intarsia works		staircases
	cabinetmaking		window frames
	rotary cut veneer		laboratory furniture & fittings
			ship, rail & truck building
			weapons industry
			blind veneer

PINK IVORY *(Rhamnus zeyheri)*

Family:	*Rhamnaceae*
Other Names:	*red ivory, mnai*
South Africa:	*umgoloti, umnini*
Mozambique:	*pau preto*

HABITAT
Pink ivory grows in the warm climate zones of southeast Africa, preferring hilly locations with sandy ground. Smaller specimens are transported to Europe and planted as ornamental trees in parks.

TREE DESCRIPTION
This tree attains a height of only some 20 m (66 ft)—30 m (98 ft) in exceptional cases—with diameters averaging 40–50 cm (1.5 ft). In Zimbabwe older trees with diameters of 80–100 cm (2.5–3.5 ft) have been found.

WOOD DESCRIPTION
The white-yellow sapwood is approximately 5 cm (2 in) thick and not usable. The core wood is pink to pinkish-red. Exposure to light will cause it to darken to an orange-brown color and take on a golden luster. Pink ivory is similar in appearance to palissandre.

Durability Class	I	**E – Module**	14,300 N/mm²
Raw density	0.90 g/cm³	**Volume dwindle**	9.5 %
Bending strength	160 N/mm²	**Tangential shrinkage**	6.0 %
Compression strength	80 N/mm²	**Radial shrinkage**	4.0 %

PROPERTIES AND APPLICATIONS

This hard, dense wood dries very slowly. It is durable, quite weather- and insect-resistant, and is moderately workable (although its hardness can prolong any procedure). Pre-drilling is recommended for operations with glue, nails, and screws. Planing can produce smooth, beautiful surfaces. Popular applications include intarsia and molding work, and usage in the flooring industry.

USES

Indoor/Outdoor

Very Good	Good	Usable	Not Usable
furniture	walls, decking	construction wood	plywood
flooring	paneling	doors	ship, rail & truck building
intarsia works	musical instruments	staircases	blind veneer
cabinetmaking	weapons industry	window frames	
rotary cut veneer		laboratory furniture & fittings	
flat sawn veneer		modeling	

SABUNI *(Gnophyllum giganteum)*

Family: *Meliaceae*

Other Names:
D.R. of the Congo: *sabuni*

HABITAT

Little is known of sabuni. It is located in the northeastern region of the Democratic Republic of the Congo, favoring the evergreen rain forest highlands where it tends to grow individually. The occasional specimen may be found growing among other deciduous tree species in other parts of Africa.

TREE DESCRIPTION

Sabuni achieves heights of up to 40 m (131 ft) with diameters of 40–70 cm (1.5–2.5 ft). The crown is spherical and comprised of a dense canopy of leaves. The trunk is straight and free of branches for up to 30 m (98 ft), and the root buttresses, which often sprout branches and leaves, can grow to 4 m (13 ft) high. The wood emits a bitter smell when sawn.

WOOD DESCRIPTION

The thin sapwood is not differentiated from the core wood, and is detached when the bark is stripped. The wood is white-yellow with a clear crystalline gloss; its appearance bears many similarities to olonvogo (*Fagara macrophylla; see separate reference*), although this is the harder wood.

Durability Class	II	E – Module	11,000 N/mm²
Raw density	0.82 g/cm³	Volume dwindle	8.8 %
Bending strength	110 N/mm²	Tangential shrinkage	-
Compression strength	-	Radial shrinkage	-

PROPERTIES AND APPLICATIONS

Sabuni has yet to undergo rigorous testing or be formally certified, but results so far indicate it to be in the tier of highest quality timbers. What is known is that it is very hard, heavy, and stable, and has been shown to be an excellent choice for flooring, intarsia and veneer works. When polished, the wood has a resplendent gloss as if emanating a light of its own, and the finished product often has a white-brown coloration like ivory. Sabuni is highly suitable for furniture production and cabinetmaking; however, it is not sufficiently weatherproof to be used for outdoor applications.

USES
Indoor

Very Good	Good	Usable	Not Usable
furniture	cabinetmaking	musical instruments	construction wood
flooring	weapons industry	doors	plywood
walls, decking	modeling	staircases	window frames
paneling			laboratory furniture & fittings
intarsia works			ship, rail & truck building
rotary cut veneer			blind veneer
flat sawn veneer			

SAPELLI / SAPELE *(Entandrophragma cylindricum)*

Family:	*Meliaceae*

Other Names:	*sapele*
Ivory Coast:	*bibitu, lotue*
Ghana:	*scented mahogany*
Nigeria:	*ubilesam, ukwekan*
Cameroon:	*bonamba*
Congo countries:	*lifaki, botsife*
Angola:	*lifuti*
Tanzania:	*miovu*
Uganda:	*muyovo*

HABITAT
Sapelli (or sapele) is a common wood found in a large habitat ranging from Sierra Leone in the west to the Democratic Republic of the Congo in the east, and to Angola in the south. It is found in both evergreen rain forests as well as areas of the savannah where conditions of high air humidity (which are favorable for growth) exist.

TREE DESCRIPTION
This large, fast-growing tree reaches imposing heights of 40–60 m (131–197 ft). The diameter is typically between 70–170 cm (2.5–5.5 ft), but trees in the Ituri region of the Democratic Republic of the Congo have been known to achieve diameters of 260 cm (8.53 ft). Sapelli trunks can be clear of branches and suitable as timber to a height of 38 m (125 ft). Root buttresses are short and underdeveloped.

WOOD DESCRIPTION
The sapwood is about 8 cm (3 in) thick and grayish-pink or pale yellow in color, clearly differentiated from the strongly-colored pink-red core wood (which later darkens upon exposure to a dark red-brown). Sapelli characteristically has a well-defined, regular striped pattern.

Durability Class	I	E – Module	11,200 N/mm^2
Raw density	0.68 g/cm^3	Volume dwindle	12.6 %
Bending strength	114 N/mm^2	Tangential shrinkage	7.0 %
Compression strength	62 N/mm^2	Radial shrinkage	5.4 %

PROPERTIES AND APPLICATIONS

Despite its hardness, sapelli is considered to be a quite workable timber. It is not very pliable, and is susceptible to the effects of weather. The wood is widely-used and has many applications. Both flat sawn and (in particular) quartersawn planes reveal an attractive wavy structure that can be used to produce decorative veneers, as well as wall and ceiling paneling. Sapelli is also used for a variety of solid-wood purposes: ship construction, furniture, staircases, and flooring. Additionally, it is employed for artistic carpentry work and the making of musical instruments (violins, for example). Local people in Africa use this wood to build canoes and other types of boats.

USES
Indoor

Very Good	Good	Usable	Not Usable
furniture	construction wood	window frames	plywood
flooring	walls, decking	laboratory furniture & fittings	weapons industry
paneling	cabinetmaking	ship, rail & truck building	blind veneer
intarsia works	doors		modeling
musical instruments	staircases		
flat sawn veneer	rotary cut veneer		

SIPO / UTILE *(Entandrophragma utile)*

Family:	*Meliaceae*

Other Names:	*utile*
Sierra Leone:	*njeli*
Ivory Coast:	*merbrou*
Nigeria:	*akuk, okeang*
Cameroon:	*assang-assie*
Congo countries:	*kalunqi, m'vovo, momboyo*
Uganda:	*muyoyu*
Kenya:	*mfumbi*

HABITAT

Sipo is frequently found in much of West and Central Africa, from Sierra Leone in the west to Uganda in the east, and as far south as Angola. This slow-growing tree thrives in shady conditions; its environment of preference is the humid broad-leafed deciduous forests of the savannah, although it is sometimes found in drier areas as well.

TREE DESCRIPTION

Sipo, with its well-formed, straight, cylindrical trunk, is among the largest trees in Africa. It can reach heights of 40–50 m (131–164 ft) or more and is clear of branches to a height of 30 m (98 ft). Trunk diameters are between 70–200 cm (2.5–6.5 ft).

WOOD DESCRIPTION

The sapwood and core wood are sharply demarcated from each other. The core wood is dark red to brown and can later darken to a brown-violet color. The medium-large pores are mostly arranged singly or in pairs, or radially in groups. The wood has fine, straight fibers and often an attractive golden luster.

Durability Class	I	**E – Module**	11,300 N/mm²
Raw density	0.56 – 0.68 g/cm³	**Volume dwindle**	10.5 – 13.3 %
Bending strength	114 N/mm²	**Tangential shrinkage**	6.8 %
Compression strength	62 N/mm²	**Radial shrinkage**	4.7 %

PROPERTIES AND APPLICATIONS

Sipo is a durable, flexible wood. It should be treated with a preservative if used for outdoor purposes. The timber has been proven in a number of applications, including ship construction, wall and ceiling paneling, various solid-wood construction projects, furniture, staircases and flooring. The wood finishes well, and it is suitable for veneering, although there is not a large demand for it.

USES

Indoor/Outdoor

Very Good	Good	Usable	Not Usable
furniture	construction wood	musical instruments	plywood
paneling	flooring	rotary cut veneer	laboratory furniture & fittings
	walls, decking	modeling	weapons industry
	intarsia works		blind veneer
	cabinetmaking		
	doors		
	staircases		
	window frames		
	ship, rail & truck building		
	flat sawn veneer		

SOUGUE *(Parinari excelsa)*

Family:	*Rosaceae*
Other Names:	*African greenheart, mubura*
Senegal:	*mampata*
Sierra Leone:	*dawe*
Ivory Coast:	*assain, catesima, mousse, piolo*
Ghana:	*afam, kotosima*
Nigeria:	*kotossouma, esagho*
Congo countries:	*pemba, bobombi, mulanga*

HABITAT

The sougue tree is broadly distributed throughout West, Central and East Africa. It flourishes in the humid evergreen forests of higher elevations, such as between 1,000–2,000 m (3,281–6,562 ft) above sea level, where it grows mainly in groups. It is frequently found in the mountainous forests of the eastern Congo and Uganda.

TREE DESCRIPTION

Sougue trees are up to 50 m (164 ft) tall and have a characteristically dense crown. The trunk is slim, cylindrical, straight, and without root buttresses; it can be clear of branches for up to 25 m (82 ft). The average trunk diameter is between 100–150 cm (3.5–5 ft).

WOOD DESCRIPTION

The sapwood and core wood are clearly distinguishable. The sapwood is yellowish-white, while the core wood is at first yellowish-brown, and then darkens after exposure to light to a deep red to chocolate-brown color. The grain is moderately interlocked.

Durability Class	III	**E – Module**	15,900 N/mm^2
Raw density	0.80 g/cm^3	**Volume dwindle**	17.9 %
Bending strength	114 N/mm^2	**Tangential shrinkage**	10.7 %
Compression strength	67 N/mm^2	**Radial shrinkage**	6.8 %

PROPERTIES AND APPLICATIONS

Sougue is fairly hard and has good mechanical strength properties. The wood is moderately durable and weather resistant. It dries slowly and quite poorly, being prone to twisting and slight cracking on the ends. Sougue is rather difficult to work with, requiring carbide- or diamond-tipped tools to cut. Its main use is for construction timber for interior and exterior works, particularly as large support beams. There currently exists only a relatively small export demand for the wood, although this may change as its best uses become better known over time. Nevertheless it is not cheap, partly because overseas carpenters find the wood's color an attractive element for decorative works.

USES
Indoor/Outdoor

Very Good	Good	Usable	Not Usable
	construction wood	flooring	plywood
	furniture	intarsia works	staircases
	walls, decking	musical instruments	window frames
	paneling	cabinetmaking	weapons industry
	doors	laboratory furniture & fittings	blind veneer
		ship, rail & truck building	modeling
		rotary cut veneer	
		flat sawn veneer	

TALI *(Erythrophleum suaveolens)*

Family:	*Caesalpiniaceae*
Other Names:	*missanda sasswood, redwatertree*
Congo countries:	*kassa, sasswood, ipomie, mwafi*
Ghana:	*potrodom*
Cameroon:	*bolondo, elong, eloun, mushenga*

HABITAT
Tali's habitat includes both the rain forests and savannah of virtually the entire African tropical zone, both north and south of the equator.

TREE DESCRIPTION
Tali is a light evergreen tree that reaches heights of up to 33 m (108 ft); specimens in the savannah tend to be shorter, mostly 15–20 m (49–66 ft) tall. The irregularly-growing trunk has a diameter of 80–120 cm (2.5–4 ft); its upper half is mostly free of branches and it has root buttresses of varying sizes. Straight trunks reveal an irregular cross section when felled.

WOOD DESCRIPTION
The core wood is yellow-, gold- or dark-reddish-brown, frequently with a green sheen, and is usually veined with wide, dark stripes. When stored for a long period of time, the wood takes on a coppery coloration with a silky shimmer. Tali has a limited number of rough pores which lend a coarseness to its texture.

Durability Class	II	**E – Module**	15,700 N/mm^2
Raw density	0.90 g/cm^3	**Volume dwindle**	14.5 %
Bending strength	142 N/mm^2	**Tangential shrinkage**	9.0 %
Compression strength	78 N/mm^2	**Radial shrinkage**	5.4 %

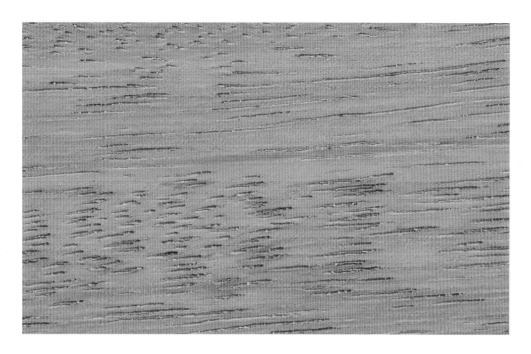

PROPERTIES AND APPLICATIONS

This solid and pliable wood has, in general, good strength properties, although compared with its heavy weight, it offers only moderate resistance to damage and collision impacts. Tali is durable and weather-resistant. The wood is difficult to process because of its hardness and irregularities but makes a good construction timber and is frequently used in water, port and bridge building projects. Furthermore, it is highly suitable for heavy-duty floors in schools, sport halls, department stores and other official buildings. Its beautiful striped pattern makes it a popular choice for fine carpentry works and veneers.

USES
Indoor/Outdoor

Very Good	Good	Usable	Not Usable
flooring	construction wood	musical instruments	plywood
walls, decking	furniture	window frames	laboratory furniture & fittings
paneling	cabinetmaking	weapons industry	blind veneer
intarsia works	doors		modeling
staircases	ship, rail & truck building		
flat sawn veneer	rotary cut veneer		

TEAK / VESAMBATA *(Oldfielda africana)*

Family:	*Euphorbiaceae*

Other Names:	*teak d'Afrique*
Sierra Leone:	*turtosa*
Liberia:	*panlei, rla, saintue*
Ivory Coast:	*dantoue*
Cameroon:	*alenile, bobino*
Congo countries:	*vesambata*

HABITAT

Teak is found in various parts of tropical West and Central Africa, including the countries of Guinea, Senegal, Sierra Leone, Cameroon, and the Democratic Republic of the Congo. The tree typically grows in damp deciduous primary forests. It is sometimes called African oak because it possesses characteristics similar to European or American oak. *Oldfielda africana* is the only teak species native to Africa and should not be mistaken for *Tectona grandis* (originally from southeast Asia). It is frequently referred to as either teak-vesambata or vesambata-teak.

TREE DESCRIPTION

Teak is a deciduous tree measuring some 36 m (118 ft) in height, with a diameter of 120 cm (4 ft). The trunk is cylindrical, with relatively small buttresses at the base; branches start appearing about 20 m (66 ft) above the ground. The bark is nearly 20 mm (1 in) thick and has a medicinal application for mouth maintenance.

WOOD DESCRIPTION

The sapwood is a maximum of 6 cm (2.5 inches) thick and is white-gray to white-red. The core-wood is gray to brown-yellow, and later darkens to a dark brown color. The wood has an even fiber; its smell and taste are very bitter.

Durability Class	I	E – Module	22,700 N/mm^2
Raw density	0.87 – 0.97 g/cm^3	Volume dwindle	16.0 %
Bending strength	175 N/mm^2	Tangential shrinkage	9.0 %
Compression strength	83 N/mm^2	Radial shrinkage	6.2 %

PROPERTIES AND APPLICATIONS

Teak is a very durable, stable, hard wood. It is generally easy to work with, although appropriate carbide-tipped tools are recommended. Quality polyurethane lacquers should be used for surface treatments. The wood is used for bridge construction, shipbuilding, temporary engineering supports for water construction (it is highly water-resistant), flooring and stairs. It is also used to create musical instruments.

USES
Indoor/Outdoor

Very Good	Good	Usable	Not Usable
construction wood	flooring	furniture	intarsia works
staircases	doors	walls, decking	plywood
ship, rail & truck building		paneling	laboratory furniture & fittings
		musical instruments	blind veneer
		cabinetmaking	
		window frames	
		weapons industry	
		rotary cut veneer	
		flat sawn veneer	
		modeling	

THUYA *(Tetraclinis articulata)*

Family:	*Cupressaceae*
Other Names:	*vernix, santrak, sandaraca*
Morocco:	*arar*
Ivory Coast:	*agru, bona, cauri*
Tunisia:	*aratree*

HABITAT
Thuya is found predominately in North Africa, particularly in Morocco, Algeria and Tunisia (it is also grown in India and Saudi Arabia). The tree often grows in conjunction with olive trees and belongs to the *Cupressaceae* tree family.

TREE DESCRIPTION
This is a small tree, rarely reaching heights of more than 15 m (49 ft); however the diameter is relatively thick—up to 60 cm (2 ft). The usable portion of the trunk is often afflicted with burls, tubercles and tree warts.

WOOD DESCRIPTION
The white sapwood is very thin. The dark reddish-brown core wood has irregular dark pore marks, finely arranged fibers, and small wavy lines, all of which combine to create a beautiful grain that is marketed with the trade name of thuya burl.

Durability Class	II	**E – Module**	-
Raw density	0.88 g/cm^3	**Volume dwindle**	15.5 %
Bending strength	-	**Tangential shrinkage**	8.5 %
Compression strength	-	**Radial shrinkage**	-

PROPERTIES AND APPLICATIONS

Thuya wood is very hard and heavy; it is also durable and resistant to insects and weather. The drying process does not involve any special handling. The wood's various deformities create nice decorative patterns for veneers and intarsia production. It is also used in solid-wood form for the manufacture of expensive, hand-made luxury furniture, which is often considered highly valuable.

USES
Indoor/Outdoor

Very Good	Good	Usable	Not Usable
furniture	flooring	walls, decking	construction wood
intarsia works	weapons industry	paneling	plywood
cabinetmaking		musical instruments	staircases
flat sawn veneer		doors	window frames
		modeling	laboratory furniture & fittings
			ship, rail & truck building
			rotary cut veneer
			blind veneer

TIAMA *(Entandrophragma angolense)*

Family:	*Meliaceae*

Other Names:	*gedu nohor*
Holland:	*lokobo*
Ivory Coast:	*lokoa popo, boka, biringui*
Nigeria:	*gedu noha*
Cameroon:	*timbi, edoussie*
Congo countries:	*ipaki, vovo, esaki, mukumi, lifaki*
Uganda:	*muyovou*
Angola:	*lifuma*

HABITAT
Tiama occupies a broad section of Central Africa, where it is frequently found in both humid evergreen forests as well as the savannah. The tree's primary territory extends from Sierra Leone in the west to Uganda in the east, and down to Angola in the south.

TREE DESCRIPTION
This large tree can attain heights of 40–50 m (131–164 ft), with up to 28 m (92 ft) of the trunk being free of branches and suitable for timber. The diameter usually measures 70–120 cm (2.5–4 ft) in thickness, although specimens in the Democratic Republic of the Congo have been known to reach a diameter of 260 cm (8.5 ft). The trunk is fairly straight and cylindrical, tending to bulge in areas. The roots extend widely over the ground.

WOOD DESCRIPTION
The sapwood is frequently over 10 cm (4 inches) thick; its white-gray to light red coloration contrasts moderately with the core wood, which is salmon-red to reddish-brown (later darkening to a deep mahogany color). The wood has a fairly porous structure. Resin rings are frequently present; in addition, the tree often grows in a twisting fashion causing distinctive decorative patterns or stripes to augment the grain.

Durability Class	II	E – Module	9,000 N/mm²
Raw density	0.56 – 0.63 g/cm³	Volume dwindle	14.2 %
Bending strength	78 N/mm²	Tangential shrinkage	7.8 %
Compression strength	48 N/mm²	Radial shrinkage	5.0 %

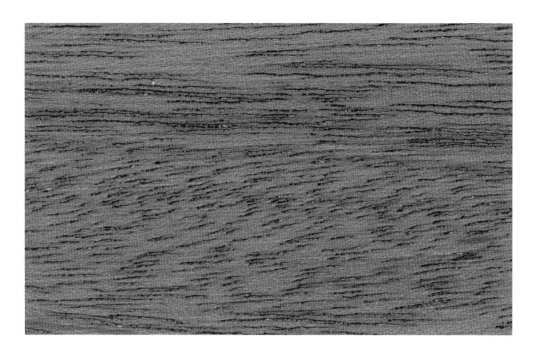

PROPERTIES AND APPLICATIONS

Tiama is very elastic and flexible, and easily takes gluing, screwing and nailing. Kiln drying must be performed with caution, as the wood has a tendency to twist when dried. The wood is suitable for veneering as well as solid-timber construction, solid-wood flooring, staircases, and for the artistic carpentry of luxury items. In England tiama is used for boat building.

USES

Indoor

Very Good	Good	Usable	Not Usable
paneling	furniture	construction wood	musical instruments
intarsia works	flooring	laboratory furniture & fittings	plywood
cabinetmaking	walls, decking	modeling	window frames
rotary cut veneer	doors		ship, rail & truck building
flat sawn veneer	staircases		weapons industry
			blind veneer

UMGUSI / MUKUSI *(Baikiaea plurijuga)*

Family:	*Ceasalpiniaceae*
Other Names:	*Rhodesian redwood, zambesi redwood, Rhodesian teak*
Angola:	*umpapa, mogoa, mohahe*
Zambia:	*mukusi, mukushi, mkusi*
Zimbabwe:	*igusi, ikusi*

HABITAT

Umgusi is located in Zambia, Zimbabwe, Botswana, Angola and Namibia. Its primary growth area is in the region around the Zambesi-Okawanga River; it mostly favors dry savannah soil.

TREE DESCRIPTION

Umgusi is a rather small deciduous tree which achieves a maximum height of approximately 18 m (59 ft); however, only about a 5 m (16 ft) section of the bole is clear of branches. A healthy mature specimen may have a trunk diameter of up to 80 cm (2.5 ft). Additional characteristics include its net-like leaves and the occasional darkly-stained trunk.

WOOD DESCRIPTION

The sapwood is up to 5 cm (2 in) thick and has a white-yellow color. The core wood is reddish-brown, darkening upon exposure to intense light to a dark red to chestnut-brown coloration. Dark wavy lines create a flame-like pattern in the grain.

Durability Class	I	E – Module	9,500 N/mm^2
Raw density	0.85 – 0.90 g/cm^3	Volume dwindle	7.8 %
Bending strength	88 N/mm^2	Tangential shrinkage	4.5 %
Compression strength	63 N/mm^2	Radial shrinkage	3.0 %

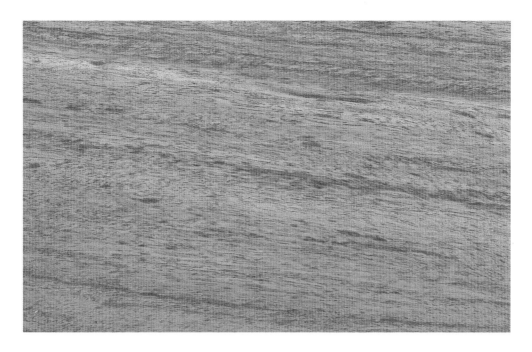

PROPERTIES AND APPLICATIONS

Umgusi is a hard, heavy wood with good physical properties. It is durable and resistant to weather and insects; however, its poor bending strength makes it rather brittle. The wood is fairly workable (similar in this regard to teak [*Tectona grandis*]), but because of its hardness, special tools are needed to cut it. Umgusi is often used to build heavy-duty flooring, for which it can have a life of over 25 years. It is used as construction timber for the building of ships and for water construction engineering.

USES

Indoor/Outdoor

Very Good	Good	Usable	Not Usable
flooring	construction wood	intarsia works	musical instruments
	furniture	laboratory furniture & fittings	plywood
	walls, decking	flat sawn veneer	doors
	paneling		window frames
	cabinetmaking		weapons industry
	staircases		rotary cut veneer
	ship, rail & truck building		blind veneer
			modeling

WAMBA *(Tessmannia africana)*

Family:	*Caesalpiniaceae*

Other Names:
D.R. of the Congo: *waka, kankoda*
Gabon: *nkaga*

HABITAT
Wamba is typically found growing in small groups in the primary rain forests of the Congo basin (Forestier Central).

TREE DESCRIPTION
This medium-large tree reaches heights between 30–50 m (98–164 ft), with diameters varying between 70–100 cm (2.5–3.5 ft). The straight-growing cylindrical trunk is clear of branches up to 30 m (98 ft); there is no above-ground rootage.

WOOD DESCRIPTION
The sapwood is pinkish- to yellowish-gray, or beige, and is approximately 10 cm (4 in) thick. It contrasts clearly with the brownish-pink to dark red core wood. A cross section of wamba discloses a decorative, alternating light and dark striped pattern on a uniform background; the same pattern and coloring are less intensively displayed on the longitudinal plane. The wood is dense with fine fibers.

Durability Class	II	**E – Module**	13,000 N/mm²
Raw density	0.80 – 0.95 g/cm³	**Volume dwindle**	14.4 %
Bending strength	140 N/mm²	**Tangential shrinkage**	-
Compression strength	70 N/mm²	**Radial shrinkage**	-

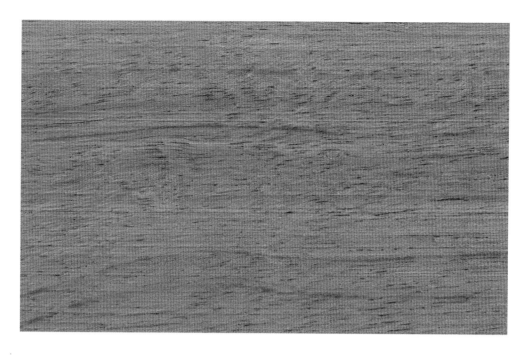

PROPERTIES AND APPLICATIONS

This hard, heavy wood possesses good compression and bending strengths. It is also durable and resistant to insects and weather; furthermore, its internal stores of resin provide protection against fungus. Wamba's favorable mechanical properties make it suitable for a variety of applications where strength is important. Among its numerous uses are the construction of factory and solid-wood floors, tool tables, staircases, window profiles, and truck platforms. It also serves as a general construction timber for both interior and exterior projects and can be used to produce works of art.

USES

Indoor/Outdoor

Very Good	Good	Usable	Not Usable
construction wood	furniture		musical instruments
flooring	paneling		plywood
walls, decking	intarsia works		blind veneer
doors	cabinetmaking		modeling
ship, rail & truck building	staircases		
	window frames		
	laboratory furniture & fittings		
	weapons industry		
	rotary cut veneer		
	flat sawn veneer		

WENGE *(Millettia laurenti)*

Family:	*Fabaceae*

Other Names:	*palissandre de Congo*
Cameroon:	*awong*
Equatorial-Guinea:	*awong*
Gabon:	*nson-so, awong*
Congo countries:	*bokonge, dikela, n'toko, koboto*

HABITAT

Wenge is a somewhat rare tree species that grows in small groups in the tropical rain forests of the central Congo basin. It is found in larger groups in the areas bordering Cameroon, Gabon and Equatorial Guinea.

TREE DESCRIPTION

This is a medium-sized tree growing up to 25 m (82 ft) in height and 60–110 cm (2–3.5 ft) in diameter. The trunk is usually straight, with a portion up to 8 m (26 ft) in length suitable as timber. Root buttresses are insignificant. The bark has a thickness between 10–12 cm (4–4.5 in) and contains a poisonous red sap.

WOOD DESCRIPTION

The white-gray sapwood is about 5 cm (2 in) thick; the core wood is dark brown to black-violet in color, with narrow brown stripes throughout, giving the wood a dual-toned appearance. The grain is straight.

Durability Class	I	**E – Module**	17,000 N/mm²
Raw density	0.85 – 1.10 g/cm³	**Volume dwindle**	10.5 – 19.5 %
Bending strength	160 N/mm²	**Tangential shrinkage**	10.0 %
Compression strength	85 N/mm²	**Radial shrinkage**	6.3 %

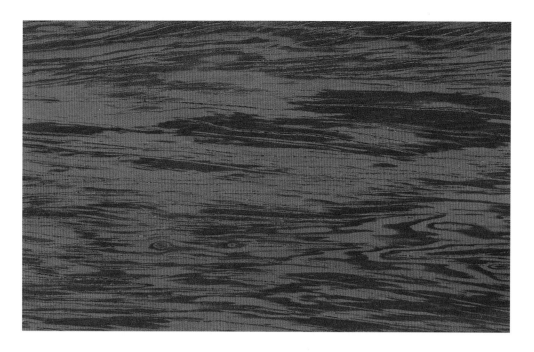

PROPERTIES AND APPLICATIONS

Wenge is a hard, heavy, flexible wood that possesses good mechanical properties. It dries slowly, and kiln drying should be done cautiously in order to reduce the incidence of cracking. Wenge is easy to cut and work with (its working properties are similar to hickory [*Carya alba*]). The wood is highly durable, as well as weather- and insect-resistant. It is much sought after in the flooring and decking industries and is in high demand for cabinetry. Wenge is also suitable as a decorative veneer but must first undergo intensive steaming.

USES
Indoor/Outdoor

Very Good	Good	Usable	Not Usable
furniture	walls, decking	construction wood	plywood
flooring	paneling	doors	ship, rail & truck building
intarsia works	musical instruments	window frames	blind veneer
cabinetmaking	staircases	laboratory furniture & fittings	modeling
rotary cut veneer	weapons industry		
flat sawn veneer			

ZEBRANO *(Microberlinia brazzavillensis)*

Family:	*Caesalpiniaceae*

Other Names: *zingana*
Cameroon: *amouk, alenele*
Guinea: *enuk enug*
Gabon: *izingana*
U.K., USA: *zebrawood*

HABITAT

Zebrano is found in tropical West-Central Africa, mainly from Cameroon to southern Gabon, but also in surrounding countries. The tree is rather rare, growing in smaller forest plots.

TREE DESCRIPTION

It can attain heights of up to 40 m (131 ft) and diameters between 50–110 cm (1.5–3.5 ft). The trunk grows straight and cylindrically, with shallow root buttresses; the bark can be up to 10 cm (4 in) thick. The tree has a large crown which, in the dry season, sprouts reddish-orange blooms.

WOOD DESCRIPTION

The white sapwood is some 15 cm (6 in) thick and unusable. The core wood is yellow- to gold-brown with intense dark brown stripes between 4–12 mm (less than .5 in) wide. The pores are filled with a resinous material. When freshly cut, the wood has a very unpleasant, ammonia-like smell; this odor gradually dissipates as the wood dries. The heartwood of older zebrano specimens is inclined to rot, and consequently logs cannot be stored for long periods of time.

Durability Class	III	E – Module	14,200 N/mm^2
Raw density	0.70 – 0.80 g/cm^3	Volume dwindle	15.0 %
Bending strength	120 N/mm^2	Tangential shrinkage	10.0 %
Compression strength	62 N/mm^2	Radial shrinkage	5.0 %

PROPERTIES AND APPLICATIONS

Zebrano is a medium-hard but very flexible wood with good physical properties. Drying is difficult and must be performed very slowly and evenly. When well-dried, the timber is highly insect-resistant. Zebrano is a popular veneer wood, although the high resin content can make handling difficult. Intensive steaming is necessary prior to flat sawn veneer processing. Zebrano is also used for cabinetmaking, moulding works, decorative panels, and the production of expensive cigar boxes.

USES

Indoor

Very Good	Good	Usable	Not Usable
flat sawn veneer	furniture	rotary cut veneer	construction wood
	paneling		flooring
	intarsia works		walls, decking
	musical instruments		plywood
	cabinetmaking		doors
	modeling		staircases
			window frames
			laboratory furniture & fittings
			ship, rail & truck building
			weapons industry
			blind veneer

TABLE OF USES

Use	Abura	Adonmoteu / Kibakoko	Aformosia	Aiele	Alepzpe	Anfiaris	Avodire	Azobe / Bongossi	Bete / Mansonia	Bilinga	Boire	Bosse Clair	Bubinga	Bumani	Cedar, East African	Cordia	Coula	Dabema	Dibetou	Difou
Modeling	G	G		G	G	U	U	G		U	U		G	G	G		U			
Blind Veneer	G	G		VG	U	VG	U			U			U	VG	G	VG	G			
Flat Sawn Veneer	G	G	G	VG	G	G	U	VG	U	G	VG	VG	U	G	VG	U	G		G	G
Rotary Cut Veneer	U	U	VG	G	G	VG	VG	U	U	U	U	U	G	G	U	G	U		VG	G
Weapons Industry	U	U	U				G		U				G	U	VG	U		U	VG	
Ship, Rail & Truck Building		G	U					VG			U	VG			G		G	VG	G	
Laboratory Furniture & Fittings	G								U	U	G				U		U			
Window Frames	U	G							U	U		G			G	U	G			
Staircases	G	G	U				G		U	U	U	G	U		G	U	G		G	
Doors	U	G	G			U			U	G	U	G	U	G	G	G		G	G	G
Plywood	VG	VG		VG	U	VG	U						U				G			
Cabinetmaking	G	G	VG		U	U	VG		G	U	VG	G	G	G	G	G	U		U	
Musical Instruments				G			G		G			G	U		U	G				
Intarsia Works	U	G	VG			U	VG		G	U	VG	U	G	VG	U	G	U		G	U
Paneling	G	G	VG		U	U	VG		G	G	G	G	G	G	VG	G	G		G	U
Walls, Decking	G	G	VG		U	U	VG		G	G	U	G	G	G	G	G	G			
Flooring	U	G	VG				VG		G	VG	G	G	U	G	G	G	U			
Furniture	G	G	VG		U		VG		G	VG	VG	VG	G	G	G	G		VG	U	
Construction Wood		G	U					VG	U	U	U	G			G	U	G	VG		
Outdoor		x	x					x				x			x	x	x	x		
Indoor	x	x	x	x	x	x	x	x	x	x	x	x	x	x	x	x	x	x	x	

Species																					
Doussie / Afzelia	x	x	VG	G	VG	G	U	G	G	U	G	G	G	VG	VG	U	G	G	U	VG	U
Ebony / Ebene d'Afrique	x	x	U	VG	G	G	VG	U	VG	VG	U	U	VG	VG	U	VG	VG	U	VG	G	VG
Effeu	x							G						G			U	U		G	G
Ekaba	x		U	U	U	U	U	G	G	U	U	U	U	G	G	U	G	G	G	G	G
Emien	x		G			U	U		U					G	U		G	U	G	G	G
Essessang	x		U	U	U	U	VG	U	G	G	U			U			U	G	U	G	VG
Essia	x	x	G	G	G	G	G	U	G			G	U	G	G	U	G	G	G	G	G
Eyong	x	x	G	G	G	G				VG	VG	G	G					U	G		
Framire	x	x	G	G	G	G	G	G	G	U	U	VG	G	G	VG	U	G	G	U	VG	G
Fuma	x			U	U	G	G	U	G	G	G			G	VG	U	G	G	G	U	G
Grenadill	x	x	U	VG	G	G	VG	U	VG	VG	VG	U	U	G	U	G	VG	VG	U	G	G
Iatandza	x		G	G	G	VG	VG	U	G	G	VG	VG	U	VG	U	U	VG	VG	VG	G	VG
Ilomba	x								U		G			U			VG	VG	G		G
Iroko / Kambala	x	x	VG	G	VG	G	G	G	VG	U	VG	VG	G	VG	G	G	VG	VG	G	U	G
Kekele	x		U	G	G	G	G	U	U	U	U		U	G	U	U	G	G	G	U	
Kele	x		U	U	U	G	G	G	G	U	U	U	G	G	G		U	G	VG	U	U
Khaya / Umbaua	x	x	G	VG	VG	G	G	U	U	VG	G	G	G	U	G	G	G	VG	VG	U	G
Khaya Cailcedrat	x	x	G	G	G	G	G	U	G	VG	VG	U	G	G	G	U	VG	VG	VG	U	G
Khaya Mahogany	x	x	U	VG	VG	G	G	U	G	VG	VG	U	G	G	VG	U	VG	VG	VG	U	G
Khaya, Acajou d'Afrique	x	x	U	VG	VG	G	G	U	G	VG	VG	U	G	G	VG	U	VG	VG	VG	G	G
Kosipo	x		U	G	VG	U	U	U	VG	VG	VG	U		G	U	U	U	U	G	U	U
Koto	x	x	U	U	U	G	G	G	U	U	U	U					G	G	G	VG	VG
Kumbi	x	x	G	U	U	G	G	G	G	G	G		U				G	G	G	VG	
Lati	x	x	U	U	U	U	U	G	U	U			U	VG	G		U	G	G	U	U
Limba	x		U	U	U	G	G	G	G	VG	G	G		G	VG	G	U	G	G	U	G

VG = Very Good   G = Good   U = Usable

193

TABLE OF USES (continued)

Use	Limbali	Longhi / Anigre	Lotofa	Madagascar-Palissandre	Makore	Mecrusse	Maobi	Movingui	Mubangu	Muhimbi	Muhuhu	Mukulungu	Muninga	Musharagi / East African Olive	Musizi	Mussibi	Mutenye	Muyati	Naga	Niangon
Modeling	U				U		U	G				U	U	G				U		U
Blind Veneer					U								U	G						U
Flat Sawn Veneer	G	VG		U	VG	G	U	G	VG	VG	G		VG	G	VG	VG	VG	G	G	G
Rotary Cut Veneer	U			U	U	G		G	G	G	U		VG	G	G	VG	G	G	G	G
Weapons Industry	U	G		U	U		U	U	G	G			VG		G			U	U	U
Ship, Rail & Truck Building	U		U			G	VG	G		VG	G	U	G	U				U	U	U
Laboratory Furniture & Fittings	U						U	VG	U	G	U		VG	U	U			U	U	U
Window Frames	G	G		U	G		U	U		U	G	G	U	U		U	G	G	G	VG
Staircases	VG	VG	U	U	U	G		G	U	G	VG	G	VG	G	G		G	G	G	VG
Doors	VG	VG	U	U	G	U	G		VG	G		VG	U	U		U	G	G	G	VG
Plywood													U	VG				U		
Cabinetmaking	G	VG	U	VG	G		U	G	G	G	G	VG	G	VG	G		G		U	U
Musical Instruments					G	G		U	U			G		U		G				
Intarsia Works	G	G	U	VG	U		U	VG	VG	U		VG	G	G	VG		G	U		U
Paneling	G	G	G	G	G		U	VG	VG	U		VG	U	VG	G		G	U	G	U
Walls, Decking	VG	G	G	G	U	U	VG	VG	U	G		VG	G	VG	G		G	G	G	U
Flooring	VG	G	G	VG	G	VG	VG	VG	VG	G		VG	G		G		G		G	
Furniture	G	G	VG	G	VG	G		G	G	G	G	VG	U		VG	G	U	G	G	U
Construction Wood	G	G	U	U	U	VG	VG	G	U	G	G	VG	VG	U		G		U	U	G
Outdoor	×			×	×	×	×		×	×	×	×	×			×	×	×	×	×
Indoor	×	×	×	×	×	×	×	×	×	×	×	×	×	×	×	×	×	×	×	×

Species																			
Niove	x		G	U	G	G			U	U	G	U	G	U	G	U	U		VG
Obeche / Abachi	x	x	U	U	G	G	U	U	G	U	G	G	VG	VG	VG	VG	VG	VG	VG
Oboto	x		G	G	VG	VG	VG	G	G	VG	U	G	G	G	G	VG	G		
Ohia	x	x	U	U	U	G	U	U	G	G	G	VG	G	U	U	U	U	U	
Okan / Denya	x		VG					VG	U	U	U	U	VG				G		
Okoume	x		U	VG	G	G	VG	U	G	G	U	U	VG	VG	VG	VG	VG	VG	VG
Olonvogo	x		G	U	U	G	G	U	G	G	G	G	U	U	G	G	G	VG	G
Onzabili	x	x	U	U	U	U	U	G	U	U	G	U	VG	G	U	U	G	VG	G
Ovengkol	x		U	G	U	G	U	G	G	U	U	U	G	G	VG	G	G	G	VG
Padouk	x	x	U	VG	G	VG	VG	VG	U	VG	G	G	VG	VG	VG	VG	VG	G	VG
Panga Panga	x	x	U	VG	VG	G	U	G	G	VG	G	U	G	G	VG	VG	VG		
Pao Rosa	x		U	G	G	G	VG	G	U	G	U	U	G	G	G	G	G		
Pink Ivory	x	x	U	VG	VG	VG	VG	G	U	VG	G	U	VG	VG	VG	G	G		
Sabuni	x		U	VG	VG	VG	VG	G	G	G	U	U	VG	VG	VG	VG	VG		VG
Sapelli	x		G	VG	VG	VG	VG	VG	G	VG	U	G	VG	VG	VG	VG	VG		
Sipo / Utile	x	x	G	VG	G	G	VG	U	G	U	G	G	G	G	G	G	G	G	VG
Sougue	x	x	G	G	U	G	U	U	U	G	U	U	VG	G	G	U	U	U	U
Tali	x	x	G	VG	VG	VG	VG	U	G	G	VG	VG	G	G	U	VG	G	U	VG
Teak / Vesambata	x	x	VG	G	U	U	U	U	G	U	U	G	VG	VG	G	U	U		VG
Thuya	x	x	U	G	G	G	VG	VG	U	U	G	U	U	G	U	G	G		U
Tiama	x		G	G	VG	VG	VG	U	G	G	G	G	VG	VG	VG	G	G	VG	U
Umkusi / Mukusi	x	x	G	VG	G	U	U	G	G	G	G	U	G	G	G	U	U		
Wamba	x		VG	G	VG	G	U	G	G	G	G	U	G	G	VG	G	G	VG	G
Wenge	x	x	U	VG	VG	VG	VG	VG	VG	VG	G	G	VG	VG	VG	VG	VG	VG	G
Zebrano	x		G	G	G	G	G	G	G	G	G	U	VG	U	U	G	VG		G

VG = Very Good G = Good U = Usable

195

BIBLIOGRAPHY

Beekman, Boerhave; W. Elsevier's Wood Dictionary in Seven Languages. Vol. 1: Commercial and Botanical Nomenclature of World Timbers; Sources of Supply; Amsterdam, Netherlands, 1964–68.

Blackwoodconservation.org; ABCP website created by James E. Harris; Tanzania.

Bolza, E. & Keating, W.G.; African Timbers, Characteristics of 700 Worldwide Species; Melbourne, Australia, 1972.

Dahms, K.G.; Holzzentralblatt, Importholz aus Afrika; DRW-Verlag; Leinfelden-Echterdingen, Germany.

Dahms, K.G.; Afrikanische Exporthölzer; DRW-Verlag; Leinfelden-Echterdingen, Germany, 1999.

Gottwald, H.; Commercial Timbers: Their Names, Determination and Description; Holzmann-Verlag; Hamburg, Germany, 1958.

ICRAF; Botanic Nomenclature for Agroforestry; ICRAF online.

Kleines Lexikon; Exotische Nutzhölzer; Deutsche Verlags-Anstalt; Stuttgart, Germany, 1965.

Lincoln, William A.: World Woods in Color; Linden Publishing, Fresno, USA, 1986, 2000.

Meyer, H.; Buch der Holznamen; M. & Schaper; Hannover, Germany, 1933.

Mühlhoff, Udo; Holz-Technik/Holzarten Web Publication; Bottrop, Germany, 1998–2002.

Parry, M. S.; Tree Planting Practices in Tropical Africa; Food and Agriculture Organization of the United Nations; 1956.

Richter, H. G. and Dallwitz, M. J.; Handelshölzer; H.G. Richter (Wood Struktur) Institute for Wood Biology and Wood Protection; Hamburg, Germany.

Sagwal, S.S.; Dictionary of Wood Technology; Vedams Books International; India, 1992.

Von Wyss & Leuenberger, A.G.; Holzarten Web Publication; Dornach, Switzerland, 1983–1993.

Wigg, L.T.; Durability of Some East African Timbers; East African Agricultural Journal, Kenya Agricultural Research Institute; Kenya, 1946.

Wimbush, S.H.; Catalogue of Kenya Timbers; Govt. Printer; Nairobi, 1950.

World of Wood Magazine; T.A.T.F., S.A. and Raleo Design S.A; USA, 1991–2003.

COMPANIES

Dara-Foret; Kotiram, John S.; Mangina, D.R. of the Congo, 2000.

Firma Fahlenkamp; C. Henning Wolters-Fahlenkamp; Bruchhausen-Vilsen, Germany, 2002.

Pentol AG; Grellingen, Switzerland, 1975.

Texwood Trading; Klemme, Rolf; Meerbeck, Germany, 2003.

Wood Floors International Inc.; Jacksonville Beach, USA, 2002.

INDEX OF COMMERCIAL NAMES

Commercial Name	Botanical Name	Family
Abachi	*Triplochiton scleroxylon*	*Sterculiaceae*
Abura	*Hallea ciliata*	*Rubiaceae*
Adonmoteu	*Antonatha fragrans*	*Caesalpinaceae*
Afrormosia	*Pericopsis elata*	*Papilionaceae*
Afzelia	*Afzelia africana*	*Caesalpiniaceae*
Aiele	*Canarium schweinfurthii*	*Burseraceae*
Alepzpe	*Albizzia coriaria*	*Mimosaceae*
Anigre	*Gambeya lacourtiana, Gambeya albida, Gambeya gigantea*	*Sapotaceae*
Antiaris	*Antiaris africana*	*Moraceae*
Avodire	*Turraeanthus africana*	*Meliaceae*
Azobe	*Lophira alata*	*Ochnaceae*
Bete	*Mansonia altissima*	*Sterculiaceae*
Bilinga	*Nauclea diderrichii*	*Rubiaceae*
Boire	*Detarium senegalense*	*Ceasalpiniaceae*
Bongossi	*Lophira alata*	*Ochnaceae*
Bosse Clair	*Guarea cedrata*	*Meliaceae*
Bubinga	*Guibourtia tessmanii*	*Ceasalpiniaceae*
Bumani	*Schrebera arborea*	*Meliaceae*
Cedar, East African	*Juniperus procera*	*Cupressaceae*
Cordia	*Cordia abyssenica*	*Boraginaceae*
Coula	*Coula edulis*	*Olacaceae*
Dabema	*Piptadeniastrum africanum*	*Mimosaceae*
Denya	*Cylicodiscus gabunensis*	*Mimosaceae*

Commercial Name	Botanical Name	Family
Dibetou	*Lovoa trichilioides*	*Meliaceae*
Difou	*Morus mesozygia*	*Moraceae*
Doussie	*Afzelia africana*	*Caesalpiniaceae*
East African Olive	*Olea hochstetteri*	*Oleaceae*
Ebene d'Afrique	*Diospyros crassiflora*	*Ebenaceae*
Ebony	*Diospyros crassiflora*	*Ebenaceae*
Effeu	*Hannoa klaineana*	*Simaroubaceae*
Ekaba	*Tetraberlinia bifoliolata*	*Caesalpiniaceae*
Emien	*Alstonia congensis*	*Apocynaceae*
Essessang	*Ricinodendron heudelotii*	*Euphorbiaceae*
Essia	*Petersianthus macrocarpus*	*Lecythidaceae*
Eyong	*Sterculia tragacantha, Eribroma oblonga*	*Sterculiaceae*
Framire	*Terminalia ivorensis*	*Combretaceae*
Fuma	*Ceiba pentandra*	*Bombacaceae*
Grenadill	*Dalbergia melanoxylon*	*Papilionaceae*
Iatandza	*Albizzia ferruginea*	*Mimosaceae*
Ilomba	*Pycnanthus angolensis*	*Myristicaceae*
Iroko	*Chlorophora excelsa*	*Moraceae*
Kambala	*Chlorophora excelsa*	*Moraceae*
Kekele	*Holoptelea grandis*	*Ulmaceae*
Kele	*Sapium ellipticum*	*Euphorbiaceae*
Khaya (Acajou d'Afrique)	*Khaya anthotheca*	*Meliaceae*
Khaya Cailcedrat	*Khaya senegalensis, Khaya grandifolia*	*Meliaceae*
Khaya Mahogany	*Khaya ivorensis*	*Meliaceae*
Khaya	*Khaya nyasica*	*Meliaceae*
Kibakoko	*Antonatha fragrans*	*Caesalpinaceae*
Kosipo	*Entandrophragma candollei*	*Meliaceae*
Koto	*Pterygota macrocarpa*	*Sterculiaceae*
Kumbi	*Lannea welwitschii*	*Anacardiaceae*
Lati	*Amphimas pterocarpoides*	*Caesalpinaceae*
Limba	*Terminalia superba*	*Combretaceae*
Limbali	*Gilbertiodendron dewevrei*	*Caesalpinaceae*
Longhi	*Gambeya lacourtiana, Gambeya albida, Gambeya gigantea*	*Sapotaceae*

Commercial Name	Botanical Name	Family
Lotofa	*Sterculia rhinopetala*	*Sterculiaceae*
Madagascar-Palissandre	*Dalbergia baroni, Dalbergia pterocarpifolia*	*Fabaceae*
Makore	*Tieghemella heckelii*	*Sapotaceae*
Mansonia	*Mansonia altissima*	*Sterculiaceae*
Mecrusse	*Androstachys johnsonii*	*Euphorbiaceae*
Moabi	*Baillonella toxisperma*	*Sapotaceae*
Movingui	*Distemonanthus benthamianus*	*Ceasalpiniaceae*
Mubangu	*Julbernardi sereti*	*Ceasalpiniaceae*
Muhimbi	*Cynometra alexandri*	*Caesalpiniaceae*
Muhuhu	*Brachylaena hutchinsii*	*Compositeae*
Mukulungu	*Autranella congolensis*	*Sapotaceae*
Mukusi	*Baikiaea plurijuga*	*Ceasalpiniaceae*
Muninga	*Pterocarpus angolensis*	*Papilionaceae*
Musharagi	*Olea hochstetteri*	*Oleaceae*
Musizi	*Maesopsis eminii*	*Rhamnaceae*
Mussibi	*Guibourtia coleosperma*	*Caesalpiniaceae*
Mutenye	*Guibourtia arnoldiana*	*Caesalpiniaceae*
Muyati	*Mildbraediodendron excelsum*	*Caesalpiniaceae*
Naga	*Brachystegia cynometroides*	*Caesalpiniaceae*
Niangon	*Heritiera utilis*	*Sterculiaceae*
Niove	*Staudtia stipitata*	*Myristicaceae*
Obeche	*Triplochiton scleroxylon*	*Sterculiaceae*
Oboto	*Mammea africana*	*Guttiferen-Clusiaceae*
Ohia	*Celtis soyauxii*	*Ulmaceae*
Okan	*Cylicodiscus gabunensis*	*Mimosaceae*
Okoume	*Aucoumea klaineana*	*Burseraceae*
Olonvogo	*Fagara macrophylla*	*Rutaceae*
Onzabili	*Antrocaryon klaineanum*	*Anacardiaceae*
Ovengkol	*Guibourtia ehie*	*Caesalpiniaceae*
Padouk	*Pterocarpus soyauxii*	*Fabaceae*
Panga Panga	*Millettia stuhlmannii*	*Fabaceae*
Pao Rosa	*Swartzia fistuloides*	*Ceasalpiniaceae*
Pink Ivory	*Rhamnus zeyheri*	*Rhamnaceae*
Sabuni	*Gnophyllum giganteum*	*Meliaceae*

Commercial Name	Botanical Name	Family
Sapelli	*Entandrophragma cylindricum*	*Meliaceae*
Sipo	*Entandrophragma utile*	*Meliaceae*
Sougue	*Parinari excelsa*	*Rosaceae*
Tali	*Erythrophleum suaveolens*	*Caesalpiniaceae*
Teak	*Oldfielda africana*	*Euphorbiaceae*
Thuya	*Tetraclinis articulata*	*Cupressaceae*
Tiama	*Entandrophragma angolense*	*Meliaceae*
Umbaua	*Khaya nyasica*	*Meliaceae*
Umkusi	*Baikiaea plurijuga*	*Ceasalpiniaceae*
Utile	*Entandrophragma utile*	*Meliaceae*
Vesambata	*Oldfielda africana*	*Euphorbiaceae*
Wamba	*Tessmannia africana*	*Caesalpiniaceae*
Wenge	*Millettia laurenti*	*Fabaceae*
Zebrano	*Microberlinia brazzavillensis*	*Caesalpiniaceae*

INDEX OF BOTANICAL NAMES

Botanical Name	Commercial Name	Family
Afrormosia elata	Afrormosia	*Papilionaceae*
Afzelia africana	Doussie / Afzelia	*Caesalpiniaceae*
Albizzia coriaria	Alepzpe	*Mimosaceae*
Albizzia ferruginea	Iatandza	*Mimosaceae*
Alstonia congensis	Emien	*Apocynaceae*
Amphimas pterocarpoides	Lati	*Caesalpinaceae*
Androstachys johnsonii	Mecrusse	*Euphorbiaceae*
Antiaris africana	Antiaris	*Moraceae*
Antonatha fragrans	Adonmoteu / Kibakoko	*Caesalpinaceae*
Antrocaryon klaineanum	Onzabili	*Anacardiaceae*
Aucoumea klaineana	Okoume	*Burseraceae*
Autranella congolensis	Mukulungu	*Sapotaceae*
Baikiaea plurijuga	Umkusi / Mukusi	*Ceasalpiniaceae*
Baillonella toxisperma	Moabi	*Sapotaceae*
Brachylaena hutchinsii	Muhuhu	*Compositeae*
Brachystegia cynometroides	Naga	*Caesalpiniaceae*
Canarium schweinfurthii	Aiele	*Burseraceae*
Ceiba pentandra	Fuma	*Bombacaceae*
Celtis soyauxii	Ohia	*Ulmaceae*
Chlorophora excelsa	Iroko / Kambala	*Moraceae*
Cordia abyssenica	Cordia	*Boraginaceae*
Coula edulis	Coula	*Olacaceae*
Cylicodiscus gabunensis	Okan / Denya	*Mimosaceae*

Botanical Name	Commercial Name	Family
Cynometra alexandri	Muhimbi	*Caesalpiniaceae*
Dalbergia baroni	Madagascar-Palissandre	*Fabaceae*
Dalbergia melanoxylon	Grenadill	*Papilionaceae*
Dalbergia pterocarpifolia	Madagascar-Palissandre	*Fabaceae*
Detarium senegalense	Boire	*Ceasalpiniaceae*
Diospyros crassiflora	Ebony / Ebene d'Afrique	*Ebenaceae*
Distemonanthus benthamianus	Movingui	*Ceasalpiniaceae*
Entandrophragma angolense	Tiama	*Meliaceae*
Entandrophragma candollei	Kosipo	*Meliaceae*
Entandrophragma cylindricum	Sapelli	*Meliaceae*
Entandrophragma utile	Sipo / Utile	*Meliaceae*
Eribroma oblonga	Eyong	*Sterculiaceae*
Erythrophleum suaveolens	Tali	*Caesalpiniaceae*
Fagara macrophylla	Olonvogo	*Rutaceae*
Gambeya albida	Longhi / Anigre	*Sapotaceae*
Gambeya gigantea	Longhi / Anigre	*Sapotaceae*
Gambeya lacourtiana	Longhi / Anigre	*Sapotaceae*
Gilbertiodendron dewevrei	Limbali	*Caesalpinaceae*
Gnophyllum giganteum	Sabuni	*Meliaceae*
Guarea cedrata	Bosse Clair	*Meliaceae*
Guibourtia arnoldiana	Mutenye	*Caesalpiniaceae*
Guibourtia coleosperma	Mussibi	*Caesalpiniaceae*
Guibourtia ehie	Ovengkol	*Caesalpiniaceae*
Guibourtia tessmanii	Bubinga	*Ceasalpiniaceae*
Hallea ciliata	Abura	*Rubiaceae*
Hannoa klaineana	Effeu	*Simaroubaceae*
Heritiera utilis	Niangon	*Sterculiaceae*
Holoptelea grandis	Kekele	*Ulmaceae*
Julbernardi sereti	Mubangu	*Ceasalpiniaceae*
Juniperus procera	Cedar, East African	*Cupressaceae*
Khaya anthotheca	Khaya (Acajou d'Afrique)	*Meliaceae*
Khaya grandifolia	Khaya Cailcedrat	*Meliaceae*
Khaya ivorensis	Khaya Mahogany	*Meliaceae*
Khaya nyasica	Khaya / Umbaua	*Meliaceae*

Botanical Name	Commercial Name	Family
Khaya senegalensis	Khaya Cailcedrat	Meliaceae
Lannea welwitschii	Kumbi	Anacardiaceae
Lophira alata	Azobe / Bongossi	Ochnaceae
Lovoa trichilioides	Dibetou	Meliaceae
Maesopsis eminii	Musizi	Rhamnaceae
Mammea africana	Oboto	Guttiferen-Clusiaceae
Mansonia altissima	Bete / Mansonia	Sterculiaceae
Microberlinia brazzavillensis	Zebrano	Caesalpiniaceae
Mildbraediodendron excelsum	Muyati	Caesalpiniaceae
Millettia laurenti	Wenge	Fabaceae
Millettia stuhlmannii	Panga Panga	Fabaceae
Mitragyna ciliata	Abura	Rubiaceae
Morus mesozygia	Difou	Moraceae
Nauclea diderrichii	Bilinga	Rubiaceae
Oldfielda africana	Teak / Vesambata	Euphorbiaceae
Olea hochstetteri	Musharagi / East African Olive	Oleaceae
Parinari excelsa	Sougue	Rosaceae
Pericopsis elata	Afrormosia	Papilionaceae
Petersianthus macrocarpus	Essia	Lecythidaceae
Piptadeniastrum africanum	Dabema	Mimosaceae
Pterocarpus angolensis	Muninga	Papilionaceae
Pterocarpus soyauxii	Padouk	Fabaceae
Pterygota macrocarpa	Koto	Sterculiaceae
Pycnanthus angolensis	Ilomba	Myristicaceae
Rhamnus zeyheri	Pink Ivory	Rhamnaceae
Ricinodendron heudelotii	Essessang	Euphorbiaceae
Sapium ellipticum	Kele	Euphorbiaceae
Schrebera arborea	Bumani	Meliaceae
Staudtia stipitata	Niove	Myristicaceae
Sterculia rhinopetala	Lotofa	Sterculiaceae
Sterculia tragacantha	Eyong	Sterculiaceae
Swartzia fistuloides	Pao Rosa	Ceasalpiniaceae
Terminalia ivorensis	Framire	Combretaceae
Terminalia superba	Limba	Combretaceae

Botanical Name	Commercial Name	Family
Tessmannia africana	Wamba	*Caesalpiniaceae*
Tetraberlinia bifoliolata	Ekaba	*Caesalpiniaceae*
Tetraclinis articulata	Thuya	*Cupressaceae*
Tieghemella heckelii	Makore	*Sapotaceae*
Triplochiton scleroxylon	Obeche / Abachi	*Sterculiaceae*
Turraeanthus africana	Avodire	*Meliaceae*